5c/ p

The Academus
RUDIMENTS PRIMER

By

R. BARRETT-WATSON
B.Mus. (DUN.), F.R.C.O.

L. McKINLAY
L.R.A.M.

and

R. HAROLD THOMSON
B.Mus. (EDIN.)

With a Preface by
W. GILLIES WHITTAKER

Adopted
as the official text-book in the
ROYAL SCOTTISH ACADEMY
OF MUSIC

LONDON
OXFORD UNIVERSITY PRESS
NEW YORK   TORONTO

Oxford University Press, Ely House, London W. 1

GLASGOW NEW YORK TORONTO MELBOURNE WELLINGTON
CAPE TOWN IBADAN NAIROBI DAR ES SALAAM LUSAKA ADDIS ABABA
DELHI BOMBAY CALCUTTA MADRAS KARACHI LAHORE DACCA
KUALA LUMPUR SINGAPORE HONG KONG TOKYO

ISBN 0 19 317304 2

A Companion to
THE ACADEMUS BOOK OF QUESTIONS ON
THE RUDIMENTS OF MUSIC
by the same authors

First edition 1933
Tenth impression 1971

PRINTED IN GREAT BRITAIN

PREFACE

Of the making of theoretical text-books there is apparently no end. It is well, however, that one may never cry 'finis', because it would mean that all originality in teaching had come to a conclusion. Nothing is more fatal to a teacher than rigidly fixed plans. A scheme there must be, otherwise instruction would be chaotic, but the skeleton must needs be clothed with living and ever-changing flesh if the organism is to be healthy.

It cannot be claimed that there is anything new or original in this text-book. It is merely the outcome of the needs of certain courses and prolonged discussions between teachers of varied age and experience. It will assuredly not suit all, but critics will find, if they try to write a similar treatise for their own use, that an elementary book is vastly more troublesome to plan and to execute than one dealing with advanced subjects. Sol-fa has been freely used throughout : as a preparation for the Staff and as a constant companion, nothing can be more helpful.

W. GILLIES WHITTAKER.

CONTENTS

CHAPTER I

SOUND

1. Music is the language of sound. Sound is produced by a vibrating body, or by the impact of a rush of air against an opening in a tube, which causes movements or waves to pass through the atmosphere or other medium. When the waves strike the eardrum, the sensation is conveyed along the aural nerve to the brain, where it is translated into sound. (Sound does not exist in the atmosphere, but only in our own consciousness. When there is no hearer there is no sound, only waves.)

2. When the vibrations are periodic, i.e. when they occur at regular intervals of time, a musical sound is produced; when they are irregular, noise is the result.

3. The commonest methods of generating these vibrations or waves for musical purposes are as follows:

(1) By a stretched string, which may be caused to vibrate, (a) by drawing a bow across it, e.g. violin; (b) by a blow, e.g. the hammer of a pianoforte; (c) by plucking, as by the fingers on the harp.

(2) By a column of air inside a tube, e.g. wind instruments and organ pipes.

(3) By means of a reed or tongue made of a flat piece of cane or metal, e.g. oboe or harmonium.

(4) By two stretched membranes forming a kind of double reed, e.g. the vocal cords which produce the human voice.

(5) By metal, or stretched parchment, when struck or rubbed, e.g. cymbals, drums, or tambourine.

4. Musical sounds may differ in four ways:

(1) They may be high or low (**Pitch**).[1]

(2) They may be long or short (**Duration**).

(3) They may be loud or soft (**Intensity**).[2]

(4) They may differ in **quality** or **character**, i.e. harsh, smooth, bright, dull, hollow, metallic, &c.[3]

---

[1] Pitch is determined by the frequency of the vibrations. The same rate of vibration always produces the same pitch, and the same wave-length. The greater the number in a given time, the higher the pitch. If the number of vibrations necessary to produce a certain pitch be doubled, the resulting sound is said to be an octave (see p. 2) higher than the original.

[2] The intensity of a sound varies according to the amplitude or width of the vibration of the sound wave.

[3] The Quality or Character (Fr. *Timbre*) depends upon the type or form of vibration, due to the presence, along with the fundamental sound, of **Harmonics or Upper Partials** (see p. 82) in varying degrees.

CHAPTER 2

THE PITCH OF SOUNDS

5. In the English language musical sounds are named in an ascending order after the first seven letters of the alphabet, A–G, these being repeated at the octaves above and below. (Octave, eight, is the term given to the next sound above or below which has the same letter name, as A–A, B–B, &c.)

(For foreign names see footnote on page 8.)

6. The pitch of these sounds is shown to the eye by a set of parallel lines with spaces between, called a **Staff** or **Stave**. The higher the line or space the higher is the pitch of the sound represented.

7. Eleven of these lines are used:

Ex. 1.

Staff lines are always numbered from the bottom upwards.

This series of eleven lines and ten spaces is called the **Great Staff,** of which the middle or sixth line is called **Middle C,** corresponding to middle C of the pianoforte, or the lowest C of the violin.

The following shows the names of all the lines and spaces:

Ex. 2.

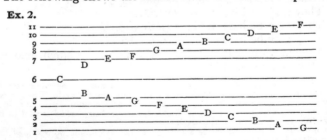

It will be noticed in the above that the five highest and the five lowest lines have been separated from the Middle C line, in order to make its position clearer to the eye.

The Great Staff being confusing to read, it is usual at the present day to select from it a small staff of five lines :

Ex. 3.

8. This staff, however, only shows the **relative** and not the **actual** pitch of the sounds, therefore it becomes necessary to have some method of indicating which portion of the Great Staff is represented by these lines. For this purpose a sign called a **Clef** is used. There are three of these clefs, which take their names from the lines of the Great Staff on which they are placed, namely, ℈ or ☙, F Clef ;

♭, G Clef ; ╫ or ╟, C Clef (derived from medieval ways of writing F, G, and C). Clef, the French word for Key, literally means a key to unlock the staff.

9. For voices or instruments of low pitch the lowest set of five lines (1–5) is used, and the sign ☙ is placed on the fourth line, showing that the name of that line is F, the F below middle C.

Ex. 4.

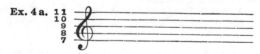

This is called the **Bass** staff. For voices or instruments of high pitch the highest set of five lines (7–11) is used, and the sign ♭ is placed on the second (eighth line of the Great Staff) line, showing that the name of that line is G, the G above middle C.

This is called the **Treble** staff.

Ex. 4 a.

10. The following are the various staffs for which the C clef is commonly used, in the order of their pitch :

> **Soprano.**
> **Mezzo-soprano.**
> **Alto.**
> **Tenor.**

The compass of each of the above voices being approximately one line (and space) lower than the one above it, the five lines selected from the Great Staff will be one line lower for each voice.

The compass of the Soprano is one line lower than the Treble, therefore the lines required for this voice are 6–10:

Ex. 5.   Soprano Staff.

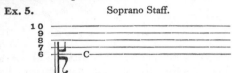

The lines required for the Mezzo-soprano are therefore one line lower than for the Soprano, 5–9, those for the Alto one line lower than for the Mezzo-soprano, 4–8, and for the Tenor one lower than for the Alto, 3–7.

Ex. 6.   Mezzo-soprano Staff.

Ex. 7.   Alto Staff.

Ex. 8.   Tenor Staff.

It will be noticed that as the compass of the voices falls, a line is taken away from above, and another added below the Middle C line, which never varies in its pitch.

11. The C clef is used at the present day for the following instruments :—Viola, 'Cello, Bassoon, Trombone, and occasionally for the Double-bass.

The following staff gives the lines required for the various voices in relation to the Great Staff :

Ex. 9.

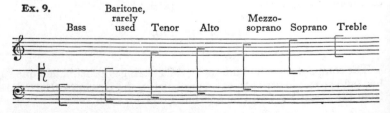

For convenience each clef is generally given the name of the staff on which it is placed—Alto clef, Bass clef, &c.

After the principle of the C clef has been grasped, an easy way to remember on which line to place the C clef is to keep in mind the order of the voices, starting with the Soprano. Thus: Soprano, clef on 1st line; Mezzo-soprano, 2nd line; Alto, 3rd line; Tenor, 4th line.[1]

It is now the custom in writing choral music in **Open Score**, i.e. where each part is written on a separate staff with its own clef, to write the Tenor part an octave higher on the **Treble staff**, and mark it

Ex. 10.

8ve lower

12. Signs called **Notes** are placed on the lines and in the spaces to indicate the pitch and duration (for duration see chap. 3) of the desired sound:

Ex. 11.

F   D   C   A

13. When sounds higher or lower than those which can be indicated by the staff are required, short lines called **Leger**[2] **lines** are employed. These can be used to any height or depth.

[1] The above gives the common modern use of the clefs. The following are found in old music:

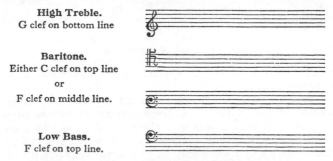

High Treble.
G clef on bottom line

Baritone.
Either C clef on top line
or
F clef on middle line.

Low Bass.
F clef on top line.

[2] Leger lines should only be long enough to accommodate a single note, otherwise the result is a virtual extension of the staff and consequent difficulty in reading.

The following are examples of Bass and Treble staffs with three leger lines above and below :

Ex. 12.

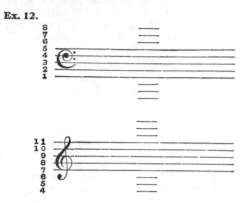

It will be noticed that the leger lines above the Bass staff are the lines 6, 7, 8 of the Great Staff, i.e. Middle C and the first two lines of the Treble staff, and that the leger lines below the Treble staff are Middle C and the 5th and 4th lines of the Bass staff.

If the second leger line or any line beyond is required, the complete number must be used. No unnecessary lines should be used.

Ex. 13.

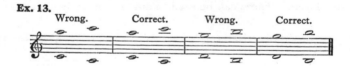

Tones and Semitones

14. The term **Interval** is applied to the difference in pitch between two sounds.

The smallest interval in common musical use is called a **Semitone,** or half a tone. A **Tone** consists of two semitones. The interval between a line and the next space of the staff is either a tone or a semitone. The interval between B and C, and between E and F is a semitone. The interval between any other two sounds with adjacent names is a tone.

15. A **Sharp** (♯) placed on a line or space raises the pitch of

that line or space one semitone, a **Flat** (♭) lowers it one semitone. If we require the sign for the sound which lies between C and D, we can write either C sharp:

Ex. 14.

or D flat:

NOTE.—A semitone such as C–C♯, where the two notes have the same letter-name, is called a *Chromatic Semitone* (see p. 80); one such as C–D♭, where the notes have different letter-names, is called a *Diatonic Semitone* (see p. 81).

The same process applies to D–E, F–G, G–A, A–B. As F is a semitone above E it is clear that E sharp is the same pitch as F, and F flat the same pitch as E. Similar relations hold between B and C.

16. If we wish to raise the pitch of a sound two semitones, the sign of a **Double Sharp** (×) is used; to lower the pitch of a sound two semitones, two flats are required (♭♭) called a **Double Flat**. If the sound has already been raised or lowered a semitone, the double sharp or double flat will raise or lower the sound **One** additional semitone only.

All signs for alteration of pitch when used in conjunction with notes must be written before the note, i.e. on the left side. We say C♯, but we write ♯C.

17. A sign called a **Natural** (♮) is used to cancel a sharp, flat, double sharp, or double flat:

Ex. 15.

When it is desired to change from a double sharp to a single sharp, either ♮♯ or ♯ may be employed. A similar method is applied to a double flat. (The single accidental in each case is preferable.)

Ex. 15 a.   better   better.

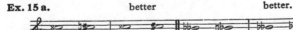

18. Sharps, flats, and naturals which occur incidentally in the course of the music are called **Accidentals**. An accidental affects only sounds of the same pitch, and in the same bar (see p. 13, par. 28), unless the sound is sustained into the next bar:

Ex. 16.

19. From the above it will be seen that every sound except that lying between G and A may be expressed in three different ways, i.e. C may be written as B sharp (a semitone above B), C, or D double flat (a tone below C), C sharp may be written as B double sharp, C sharp, or D flat, &c.

This use of different letter-names for sounds of the same pitch, as above, is called **Enharmonic**.

The following shows the names of all the notes in the four languages most generally used for musical terms:

English.	German.	French.	Italian.
C	C	Ut	Do
C flat	Ces	Ut bémol	Do bemolle
C sharp	Cis	Ut dièse	Do diesis
D	D	Re	Re
D flat	Des	Re bémol	Re bemolle
D sharp	Dis	Re dièse	Re diesis
E	E	Mi	Mi
E flat	Es	Mi bémol	Mi bemolle
E sharp	Eis	Mi dièse	Mi diesis
F	F	Fa	Fa
F flat	Fes	Fa bémol	Fa bemolle
F sharp	Fis	Fa dièse	Fa diesis
G	G	Sol	Sol
G flat	Ges	Sol bémol	Sol bemolle
G sharp	Gis	Sol dièse	Sol diesis
A	A	La	La
A flat	As	La bémol	La bemolle
A sharp	Ais	La dièse	La diesis
B	H	Si	Si
B flat	B	Si bémol	Si bemolle
B sharp	His	Si dièse	Si diesis

In German the double sharp is denoted by the addition of *isis,* and the double flat by *eses* to the letter, e.g. *Gisis, Geses.* The French and the Italians use the words *double* and *doppio* respectively, e.g. *Fa double bémol, La doppio diesis.*

CHAPTER 3

THE DURATION OF SOUNDS

20. LENGTH or duration of sound is shown by signs of different shapes called **Notes**; periods of silence by signs called **Rests**.

21. The Semibreve or Whole-note is in modern times taken as the standard from which the value of all other notes is calculated.

22. The following table gives the relative lengths of the various notes in general use, and the rests of corresponding value:

NOTE.		REST.	VALUE IN TERMS OF A SEMIBREVE.
Breve	‖○‖ or ▭	I	2
Semibreve	○	▬	1
Minim	♩	▬	$1\frac{1}{2}$
Crotchet	♩	♪ or ⌐	$\frac{1}{4}$
Quaver	♪	┐	$\frac{1}{8}$
Semiquaver	♬	┐	$\frac{1}{16}$
Demisemiquaver	♬	┐	$\frac{1}{32}$

(For foreign names see footnote on p. 12.)

For notes or rests of smaller value than the above, $\frac{1}{64}$, $\frac{1}{128}$, &c., hooks are added as required, each additional hook reducing the note or rest to half its value.

The Breve is most commonly found in Church music.

It will be seen that each note or rest is double the value of that which follows (e.g. a semibreve is equal to two minims).

23. Quavers and notes of shorter value may either be written separately or grouped together by joining the strokes:

Ex. 17.

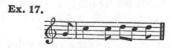

This grouping does not affect the value of the notes, nor does the position of the stems, which may be turned either up or down. When a single line of melody is written on a staff, the stems of single notes lying above the middle line are turned down, those below are turned up. Those on the middle line may be turned either way. Where quavers or shorter notes are grouped together, all the stems are turned in the same direction, and, generally speaking, the stems are kept within the staff. When the stem is turned up it is placed at the right side of the note, when below at the left. All hooks not grouped are turned to the right:

Ex. 18.

24. Where two melodies are written simultaneously on the same staff, the notes of the upper melody have their stems turned up, and those of the lower one down:

Ex. 19.

25. Notes of any kind may be lengthened in three ways:

(1) By joining together two of the same pitch by means of a curved line called a **Tie** or **Bind**  The first note only is sounded and sustained for its own value together with that of the following tied note; thus the value of the second note is added to that of the first. This method may be applied to any number of notes.

(2) By placing one or more **Dots** after the note, the first dot adding half the value of the note, and each succeeding dot adding half the value of the one before it, e.g.

(3) By placing over the note the sign ⌢, called a **Pause**, which prolongs the sound to a length which is left to the discretion of the performer.

(2) and (3) also apply to rests.

26. A note may be shortened by the use of a **Staccato** (detached) mark, which is placed at the head of the note. There are three kinds in general use.

(1) **Staccato** (short), which decreases the value of the note by one-half:

Ex. 20.   Effect.

(2) **Mezzo-staccato** (rather short), which decreases the value of the note by one quarter:

Ex. 21.　　　　　　　　　Effect.

Mezzo-staccato is also indicated by ⁔ placed over the note.

(3) **Staccatissimo** (very short), which decreases the value of the note by three-quarters:

Ex. 22.　　　　　　　　　Effect

The sign ⁓, called **Tenuto,** indicates that care must be taken to hold the note on which it is placed for its full value.

As a general rule the size of crotchet rests and those of less value should be about half that of the corresponding note. Care should be taken to place them as near the centre of the staff as possible (*a* and *b*), unless two or more melodies are written on the same staff, in which case the position of the rests must make clear to which part they belong (*c* and *d*).

(*a*)　　　　　　　Ordinary position.

(*b*)　　　　　　　Ordinary position.

(*c*)　　　　　　　Two parts.

(*d*)　　　　　　　Three parts.

In writing music it is well to acquire a good style from the first. To try to imitate printed music is both unnecessary and undesirable. Time should not be wasted in making the outlines of crotchet heads and filling them in by circular movements of the pen. One stroke with a soft broad-nibbed pen held slantwise is sufficient. Stems should be joined to the heads, and should be straight and at right angles to the staff lines. Another important point is the spacing of the notes, especially where there are two or more moving parts on the same staff:

NOTE.—The following shows the names of notes in English, with foreign equivalents. In America the method of naming follows the German custom: Semibreve = Whole-note, Minim = Half-note, &c.

	English.	*German.*	*French.*	*Italian.*
	Breve	*Brevis*	*Carrée*	*Breve*
	Semibreve	*Takt-note*	*Ronde*	*Semibreve*
	Minim	*Halb-note*	*Blanche*	*Bianca*
	Crotchet	*Viertel-note*	*Noir*	*Nera*
	Quaver	*Achtel-note*	*Croche*	*Croma*
	Semiquaver	*Sechzehntel-note*	*Double-croche*	*Semicroma*
	Demisemi-quaver	*Zweiunddreis-sigstel-note*	*Triple-croche*	*Semi-bis-croma*

CHAPTER 4

ACCENT AND TIME

27. In listening to music it will be noticed that there is a steady throb to which one could march or clap. This is called the **Pulse** or **Beat**. It will also be observed that some beats are stronger than others. This stress given to certain notes more than to others is termed **Accent**. Again, it will be observed that the accent falls regularly, so grouping the sounds into sets as to produce what is called **Time** or **Metre**.

28. These sets may contain one strong and one weak beat, or one strong and two weak beats.

Ex. 23. (a)

(b)

The number of beats from one regular or periodic accent up to but not including the next is called a **Measure** (also called a **Bar**). If there are two beats to each measure, as at (a), we have **Duple** time; if three beats, as at (b), **Triple** time.

29. In order to show which of the notes have to be accented, a line called a bar-line is placed across the stave immediately before each accented note:

Ex. 24. (a)

(b)

30. We frequently find measures containing four beats, called **Quadruple** time. This kind of time, however, is really made up

of two measures of duple, one of which is stronger than the other, the bar-line showing which is the stronger measure. In quadruple time, therefore, the first beat is strong, the second weak, the third medium, and the fourth weak.

Ex. 25.

31. When two bar-lines are placed close together they are called a **Double Bar**. The double bar does not indicate accent unless it replaces an ordinary bar-line. Its function is to mark off an important division of a movement, and it may be placed in any position in a measure.

32. Any note may be taken as a beat, but the commonest are the Minim (half-note), Crotchet (quarter-note), and Quaver (eighth-note).

33. The various kinds of time are expressed by the use of two figures placed one above the other on the staff. This sign is called the **Time-signature**.

Where an undotted note is a beat, the upper figure gives the number of beats in the bar, and the lower represents the kind of note which is used as a beat, in terms of a fraction of a semibreve— half-note, quarter-note, &c.

Ex. 26.

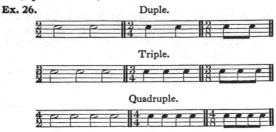

34. In all the foregoing times each beat may be normally divided into two or four parts, e.g. ♩ ♩ = ♫ ♫, and when this is the case the time is said to be **Simple**.

35. Sometimes, however, each beat of the bar is divisible into three parts, and when this is the case the time is called **Compound**.

Above are two beats, each divided into three parts, so that each whole beat must now be shown by a note equal to three quavers, i.e. a dotted crotchet. From this it will be seen that the top figure of the time-signature *should* be 2 (since there are two beats), and the lower figure 4 dotted (since each beat is a dotted crotchet), thus—

$$\frac{2}{4} \cdot \quad \text{♫♪♪ ♫♪♪} \mid \text{♩.} \quad \text{♩.} \quad \|$$

36. Unfortunately, however, compound time-signatures are not shown in the same way as simple time. As each beat is normally divided into three, the top figure indicates the number of beats in the bar multiplied by 3. Thus in the above example there are two beats each divided into three parts, so that the top figure is $2 \times 3 = 6$, showing six divisions; while the lower figure shows the value of each division, which is a quaver, therefore the lower figure is 8. Thus the time-signature is $\frac{6}{8}$. It is important to remember that there are not six beats in the bar, but two dotted crotchet beats, each divisible into three parts, i.e. Compound Duple time.

In $\frac{2}{4}$, $\frac{3}{4}$, and $\frac{4}{4}$ a ♩. is a beat and a half, but here it is **one** beat.

37. The following will illustrate the method of constructing Simple and Compound time-signatures :—

Triple time in minims.	*Simple.*	Triple time in dotted minims.	*Compound.*
	Three beats in a bar, therefore top figure will be 3. Each beat is shown by a ♩ therefore lower figure is 2. The time-signature is thus $\frac{3}{2}$.		Three beats in a bar, but each is divided into three parts, therefore top figure is $3 \times 3 = 9$. Each division is shown by a ♩ therefore lower figure is 4. The time-signature is thus $\frac{9}{4}$.

All other time-signatures are constructed similarly.

38. More unusual time-signatures sometimes occur in modern music, such as $\frac{5}{4}$, $\frac{7}{4}$, $\frac{15}{8}$. These will generally be found to be combinations of two or more simple or compound times, $\frac{5}{4}$ being a bar of $\frac{2}{4}$ alternating with one of $\frac{3}{4}$ or vice versa; $\frac{15}{8}$ (five dotted crotchets in a bar) a similar combination in compound time; $\frac{7}{4}$ a bar of $\frac{3}{4}$ alternating with one of $\frac{4}{4}$.

$\frac{4}{4}$-time is often expressed by the sign C, sometimes called **Common Time,** though the C does not represent the initial letter of the word ' common '. In medieval times triple time was regarded as perfect, and was represented by a circle ○, a sign of perfection. Measures containing two or four beats were considered imperfect, and to express these times the circle was broken, giving it the shape of the letter C.

The sign ₵ is used to express both $\frac{2}{2}$ and $\frac{4}{2}$ times. The former is usually called **Alla Capella,** and the latter **Alla Breve** time. In these cases the beat is always represented by a minim.

In Sol-fa notation the following method of indicating bars and pulses is used, the space occupied by a pulse being always the same throughout a line, and, if possible, throughout an entire number :

Simple Duple | : | Simple Triple | : : |

Simple Quadruple | : | : |

Compound Duple | : : | : : |

Compound Triple | : : | : : | : : |

Compound Quadruple | : : | : : | : : | : : |

Notes are sustained for the value of the spaces they occupy ; continuation is shown by horizontal lines :

| d :d | d :— | d :— | — :— ‖

Equivalent in staff $\frac{2}{4}$

Half pulses are indicated by dots, quarters by commas :

| d .d   :d ,d .d ,d | d   .d ,d :d ,d .d ‖

When the division of a beat is $\frac{3}{4} \frac{1}{4}$, the dot is shifted to the right, close to the comma:

|d   .,d :d   .,d ‖

Other combinations are:

|d ,d .– :d ,d .–,d ‖ |d .d :–.d ‖

Triplets are indicated by inverted commas:

|d ‚d ‚d :d ‚– ‚d |d ‚d ‚– :d ‚d ‚d ‖

In compound time the beat is always divided into thirds:

Compound duple.

|d :– :– |d :d :d |d :– :d |d :d :– ‖

&c.

Rests are indicated by leaving spaces blank:

|d : |d :– . | .d :d . |d .,d:d,.d ‖

Each line of the music must begin with a bracket, followed by the pulse sign concerned.

The end of a line never has a pulse sign, as this always *precedes* the note.

$$\left\{ \left\| d \quad :\text{m}.\text{r} :\text{d} \ \middle| l \quad :-.s:f \ \middle| \text{m} \quad :\text{s} \quad :1 \right\} \right.$$

$$\left\{ \left\| t \quad :r^1 \quad :-.t \ \middle| d^1.1:\text{s}.f:\text{m}.\text{r} \ \middle| d \quad :- \quad :- \right\| \right.$$

The double bar line is only used to complete a section or at the end of the movement.

A pulse unit is always the same in simple time $\left| \quad ^1_\cdot \quad \cdot \quad ^2 \quad \right\|$ and in compound time $\left| \quad \cdot \ \cdot \quad ^1 \middle| \ \cdot \ \cdot \quad ^2 \quad \right\|$

This does away with the necessity for time-signatures.

Grouping of Notes

39. When notes shorter than a crotchet are used, it is usual in instrumental music, and sometimes in vocal music, to group together as many of these as belong to the same beat, in order to make them easier to read, e.g.

Ex. 27.

In (*a*) the beat is a crotchet, therefore the total value of the notes grouped together is equal to a crotchet; in (*b*) the beat is a minim, in (*c*) a dotted crotchet, and in (*d*) a dotted quaver; therefore the total value of the notes grouped together is equal to a minim, a dotted crotchet, and a dotted quaver respectively.

40. The following exceptions to the above rule are commonly observed:

(*a*) Where there is a complete bar of quavers in ¾ time, or semi-quavers in ⅜ time, the notes are usually grouped together, e.g.

(*b*) In 4/4 time, when the first or second half of the bar consists of quavers, or in 4/8 time of semiquavers, the notes belonging to each half may be grouped together, e.g.

The following is not normally used, but sometimes the easier grouping is departed from in order to indicate phrasing:

41. In vocal music the grouping of notes depends upon the syllables allotted to them:

Ex. 28.

At (*d*) and (*e*) two different methods of writing ♪ ♫ ♫ ♪ are given. Both are correct, but the last example makes the divisions of the bar clearer to the singer.

42. If in simple time a sound is of greater value than one beat, it may where possible be represented by either a dotted note or a simple note equal to the total value of the sound : [1]

In compound time, however, the sound must be equal to two or four *complete* beats before it can be represented by one note :

In compound triple time no single note can be used for a whole bar.

Use of Rests

43. A complete bar of silence in any kind of time (except $\frac{4}{2}$) is always expressed by a semibreve rest, e.g.

Ex. 29.

In Alla Breve time ($\frac{4}{2}$) a breve rest (equal to four minims) is used : $\frac{4}{2}$ ⊐⊏ ‖

44. In the case of a complete half-bar at either end in quadruple time the two beats are represented by one rest :

Ex. 30.

45. In all other cases, when completing a bar with rests, no rest of greater value than *one* beat should be used :

Ex. 31.

   (*a*)   (*b*)   (*c*)

In (*a*) and (*b*) the beat is a crotchet, therefore two separate crotchet rests must be added. In (*c*) the beat is a dotted crotchet, therefore two separate dotted crotchet rests must be added.

---

[1] Occasionally the dot is used across a bar-line to prolong a sound into the next bar. This method was commonly in use in the seventeenth and eighteenth centuries, but gradually gave way to the use of ties. It has been revived, however, in recent years by Brahms. As the practice has not been generally adopted, the student is recommended not to use it.

BRAHMS.

46. It may be further noted that each beat or **portion of a beat** must first be completed before proceeding to the next, e.g.

Ex. 32.

Here the semiquaver, which is a quarter of a beat, must first be made up to a half-beat by the addition of a semiquaver rest, and then be made up to a whole beat by the further addition of a quaver rest, i.e. a half-beat. The last crotchet beat of the bar is completed in the same way, working backwards from the note.

47. In compound time a similar method is adopted, e.g.

Ex. 33.

Here the beat being equal to three quaver divisions, the semi-quaver at the beginning must first be made up to one quaver, then to two quavers, and so on until the beat is completed.

It should be noted in the above that the first two beats are completed by the addition of two quaver rests, whereas in the third beat a single crotchet rest is used to show the first two divisions. The reason for this is that it has become a matter of custom to use a single rest for the first $\frac{2}{3}$ of a beat, e.g.

This rule is justified by common usage, but the converse, where the rest comes at the end of the beat, is not acceptable:

Not good

Syncopation

48. When the normal accent of a bar is disturbed by a strong note falling on a weak part of the bar, the effect is called **Syncopation**. This effect may be obtained in various ways, the commonest being produced by sounding the note on a weak beat before that having the normal accent, and continuing it over the accented beat. The resulting sound is always stronger than that of the normal accent:

Ex. 34. (a) BEETHOVEN.

(b) BEETHOVEN.

A similar effect is produced when the accented note is preceded by a rest, or a note shortened by staccato:

Ex. 35.

The method of using the dot referred to in the footnote on page 20 is occasionally employed for the same purpose:

Ex. 36.

Irregular Groups

49. It has been pointed out that the normal division of a beat in simple time is into halves and quarters, and in compound time into thirds and sixths. It is often desired, however, to use other divisions of a beat. In simple time we may have thirds, fifths, sixths, sevenths, ninths, &c., and in compound time halves, quarters, fifths, sevenths, &c. For these cases (called **Irregular Groups**) a special method of writing is used which does not necessitate new kinds of notes, but uses the old ones for fresh purposes. For example, if it is desired to divide a crotchet into thirds, the notes are written as halves and the figure 3 added to indicate that their value is different from normal. An Irregular Group may therefore be defined as the division of a beat or portion of a beat into a greater or lesser number of parts than the normal.

50. The following are a few examples. It will be noticed that groups may consist of notes and rests combined.

Duplet. Two notes played in the time of three of the same kind:

Ex. 37.

Triplet.   Three notes played in the time of two of the same kind:

Quadruplet.   Four notes played in the time of six of the same kind:

Quintuplet.   Five notes played in the time of four or six of the same kind:

Sextuplet (Sextolet). Six notes played in the time of four of the same kind. (The six are divided into three groups of two.)

Ex. 41.

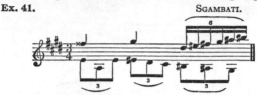

Many cases will be found where a Sextuplet has been incorrectly written where the intended effect is obviously two triplets. The following is an example:

Septolet or **Septimole.** Seven notes played in the time of four or six of the same kind:

$7=4$

Ex. 42. (*a*)

$7=6$

(*b*)

51. Many examples of incorrect notation are to be found in published works. The following are a few:

Ex. 43. (*a*)

(*b*)

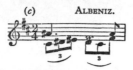

At (*a*) the two crotchets forming the Duplet should obviously be quavers, and at (*b*) the Quadruplet of quavers should be semiquavers. At (*c*) the notation should be :

52. In the time of Bach and Handel the value of the dot after a note varied. In the following example the semiquaver is played at the same time as the third of the three quavers forming the triplet :

Ex. 44.   BACH.

CHAPTER 5

SCALES

53. A SUCCESSION of sounds progressing alphabetically, each sound having a definite relationship with the starting-note, is called a **Scale.**

54. There are in general use two types of scale : those with seven different sounds to the octave, and progressing by both tones and semitones, and those with twelve different sounds to the octave, and therefore progressing entirely by semitones.

The former are called **Diatonic** scales, and in staff notation the first seven letters of the alphabet are used consecutively in naming the notes. The latter, having twelve sounds distributed over the seven letters, require the use of the same letter twice on five occasions. These are called **Chromatic** scales.

55. There are two kinds of Diatonic scale, **Major** and **Minor,** and three kinds of Minor scale, **Old** or **Modal, Harmonic,** and **Melodic.**

Major Scales

56. The scale starting from the note C, using the white keys of the piano, is the pattern on which major scales are formed. It is called the natural scale because no sharps or flats are required :

Ex. 45.

It will be found a great help in all cases to associate the notes of the scale with the Tonic Sol-fa names—Doh, Ray, Me, Fah, Soh, Lah, Te, Doh¹ (see note on p. 36).

57. The above scale will be seen to contain five tones and two semitones, arranged in such an order that it divides into two halves, each having exactly the same pattern as the other. These two halves of the scale, each containing four notes, are called **Tetrachords** (tetra = four).

58. We have noted that C D E F G A B C¹ corresponds with **d r m f s l t d¹**. The distance between any two consecutive notes is a tone, except between **m–f** (E–F) and **t–d¹** (B–C), which are semitones. Only when the major scale is constructed upon

this order of tones and semitones can it be correct. We may take any note as **doh** and sing the scale; but if, using only the white keys, we play upwards on the piano from any note except C, we find that the sounds produced do not correspond with those obtained by the sol-fa syllables, because only with C as **doh** do the semitones come in the right places.

The Sharp Scales

59. Let us now take **soh**, G of the scale of C, and regard it as a new **doh**, singing the scale upwards while playing the notes on the piano; we find that one note, F, is wrong, and that F sharp must be used instead, to bring the semitone between **te** and **doh**¹. Thus we get the scale of G major as follows:

Ex. 46.

d   r   m   f   s   l   t   d¹

60. If we now regard **soh** of the scale of G as a new **doh**, and begin a scale on D, keeping to exactly the same notes as in the previous scale of G (that is, including the sharpened F), we again find that the seventh note is wrong, and must be raised from C to C sharp to bring the semitone between **te** and **doh**¹:

Ex. 47.   D major.

d   r   m   f   s   l   t   d¹

61. Proceeding on the same principle, if we use A, E, B, F sharp, C sharp successively as **doh**, we require the sharps of the previous scale plus a new sharpened note for **te**.

62. Six facts are apparent from this:

(1) The **soh** of each scale becomes the **doh** of the next scale in the series, therefore,

(2) The order of sharp scales is G D A E B F♯ C♯.

(3) The upper tetrachord of each scale becomes the lower tetrachord of the next scale in the series.

(4) The sharps from each scale must be retained in the next of the series.

(5) The new sharp is always **te**.

(6) As we progress from the scale of C with no sharps to that of C sharp with seven, the sharps are added in the order F C G D A E B, and each is *five* degrees above, or *four* degrees below, the preceding. This is *not* the order in which the sharps occur in the scale, but that in which they are added in the series. It is also the order used in writing key-signatures (see p. 29). It is termed *the order of sharps*.

The Flat Scales

63. The series of flat scales can be worked out by taking **fah** as the new **doh**, instead of **soh** as in the sharp scale series. It will be found that the note requiring alteration is the 4th degree. This needs to be lowered to produce the semitone **me–fah**.

Ex. 48.   (a)   F major.

d   r   m   f   s   l   t   d¹

(b)   Bb major.

d₁   r₁   m₁   f₁   s₁   l₁   t₁   d

64. The following facts are apparent from this:

(1) The **fah** of each scale becomes the **doh** of the next scale in the series, therefore,

(2) The order of flat scales is F Bb Eb Ab Db Gb Cb.

(3) The lower tetrachord of each scale becomes the upper tetrachord of the next scale in the series.

(4) The flats from each scale must be retained in the next of the series.

(5) The new flat is always **fah**.

(6) As we progress from the scale of C with no flats to that of Cb with seven, the flats are added in the order B E A D G C F, and each is four degrees above, or five degrees below, the preceding. This is *not* the order in which the flats occur in the scale, but that in which they are added in the series. It is also the order used in writing key-signatures (see p. 29), and it is termed *the order of flats*.

65. In the following diagram the order of sharp scales is shown on the outside, and the order of flat scales on the inside of the circle, the two series going in contrary directions:

Ex. 49.

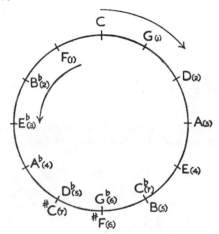

66. It will be seen that the last three scales of one series overlap with the last three of the other. That is, the scale of D♭ has the same position as C♯, G♭ as F♯, and C♭ as B. A similar correspondence is found on the piano keyboard, that is, the scales of D♭ and C♯ have notes of the same pitch but the names are different. The scale of D♭ is therefore said to be the enharmonic of C♯ (see p. 8). Similarly, the scale of G♭ is the enharmonic of F♯, and C♭ of B.

Key-signatures

67. In order to avoid the use of too many sharps or flats, as would happen if they were all inserted in the course of the music, the sharps or flats necessary to produce the particular scale required are placed together on the staff immediately after the clef. (It must be understood that, although a sharp or flat so placed appears on only one particular line or space, all the sounds bearing the same name at any octave above or below are affected by it.) This group of sharps or flats is called the **Key-signature.**

68. The following is a table of key-signatures for all the sharp keys, with the starting or key-note of each, the sharps being added in the 'order of sharps' (see p. 28):

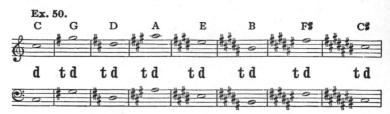

69. The following is a table of key-signatures for all the flat keys, the flats being added in the 'order of flats' (see p. 28).

The following table gives all the key-signatures as written with the Soprano, Mezzo-Soprano, Alto, and Tenor Clefs:

SHARP KEYS

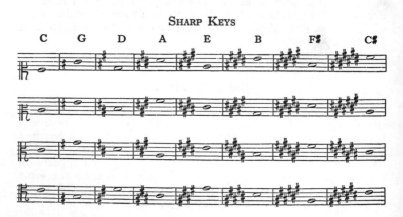

FLAT KEYS

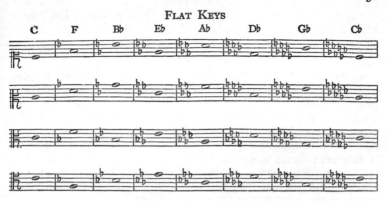

The Minor Scale

70. We found that the major scale formed a series of notes corresponding to **d r m f s l t d¹**. If, instead of beginning on **doh** we begin on **lah**, we obtain what is called the **Minor Scale**, **l t d¹ r¹ m¹ f¹ s¹ l¹**. The scale beginning on **lah** is called the **Relative Minor** of that beginning on **doh**: the scale of A minor is therefore the relative minor of C major:

Similarly, every major scale has its relative minor, so called because both have the same key-signature.

It will be noticed that, just as in major scales, the last sharp in the key-signature is always **te,** and the last flat always **fah.**

71. As was stated on p. 26, there are three forms of the Minor scale, (*a*) Old or Modal, (*b*) Harmonic, (*c*) Melodic.

Old Minor

72. This scale contains exactly the same notes as its relative major, the only difference being that the major ranges between **doh** and **doh¹**, whereas the minor ranges between **lah** and **lah¹**. The minor scales shown above in Par. 70 are therefore in the Old form.   It should be noticed that, though the two semitones still occur between the same sol-fa notes, their position in the scale order is different: in the major they occur between the 3rd and 4th and the 7th and 8th degrees, but in the Old minor they come between the 2nd and 3rd and 5th and 6th degrees, and it is this which produces the difference in the musical effect.

Harmonic Minor

73. The Harmonic minor scale contains the same notes as the Old with the exception of the seventh degree, **soh**.   This is always raised a semitone by a natural, sharp, or double sharp, according to circumstances, thus creating a semitone, **se–lah** (see note on p. 34), between the seventh note and the octave.   This alteration is made in order to produce more satisfactory harmonies, hence the name Harmonic minor.   The ♮, ♯, or × used for this purpose is never included in a key-signature, but is placed in front of the note as it occurs in the music.

Ex. 54.

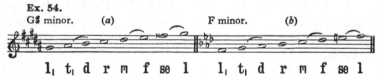

G♯ minor.   (*a*)   F minor.   (*b*)

l₁ t₁ d r m f se l   l₁ t₁ d r m f se l

There are, therefore, three semitones in the Harmonic minor scale, between 2nd and 3rd, 5th and 6th, 7th and 8th degrees.

Melodic minor

74. The leap from **fah** to **se** is an awkward and difficult one to sing in tune.   In order to avoid this we use the third form of minor scale, the Melodic.   Here, both 6th and 7th degrees are raised in the ascending scale, and restored to their original position in the descending:

Ex. 55.

(*a*)

G♯ minor.

l₁ t₁ d r m ba se l s f m r d t₁ l₁

(*b*)

F minor.

l₁ t₁ d r m ba se l s f m r d t₁ l₁

The sol-fa name for the 6th degree of the ascending melodic minor is **ba**, pronounced **bay**. In this context the sharpened **fah** is a diatonic note, and is called **ba** in order to distinguish it from **fe**, the sharpened **fah** of the major mode, which is a chromatic note (see p. 80) and produces a totally different mental effect.

It will be noticed that in the ascending scale the semitones occur between the 2nd and 3rd, and 7th and 8th degrees, but in the descending scale between the 5th and 6th, and 2nd and 3rd.

75. The terms major and minor, as applied to scales, derive their significance from the fact that, in the major scale the distance between the first and third degrees is one semitone larger than the corresponding distance in the minor scale, major meaning greater, minor meaning less.

76. It has been noticed above that scales having the same key-signatures are called **Relative major** and **minor**, e.g. C major and A minor, F minor and A♭ major. The scales starting on the same key-note, however, are called **Tonic major** and **minor** (see Par. 77), e.g. C major and C minor, F minor and F major.

77. Each degree of a diatonic scale has a name describing its position in the scale. The first degree, which is also the most important, is called the **Tonic** or **Key-note**. The two next in importance are the **Dominant** (so called because it dominates the key), five notes above the Tonic, and the **Subdominant** (or the dominant below), five notes below the Tonic. The **Mediant** (middle) lies midway between the Tonic and Dominant, and the **Submediant** midway between the Tonic and Subdominant (below). The second degree is called the **Supertonic** (above the Tonic); and the seventh degree is the **Leading-note,** so called because the tendency of the sound is to lead the ear to expect the Tonic.

Major		*Minor*
doh¹	8. Tonic	lah
te	7. Leading-note	se or soh
lah	6. Submediant	fah or **ba**
soh	5. Dominant	me
fah	4. Subdominant	ray
me	3. Mediant	doh
ray	2. Supertonic	te₁
doh	1. Tonic	lah₁

Chromatic Scales

78. When a scale proceeds entirely by semitones (unlike a Diatonic scale, which progresses in a certain order of tones and semitones), it is called **Chromatic** (see p. 80).

79. The Chromatic scale is formed by the division of the octave into twelve semitones. As there are only seven letters of the alphabet available for naming these twelve notes, it follows that five of the letters have to be used twice, and the remaining two letters once.

80. There are in common use two forms of writing the Chromatic scale, the **Harmonic,** which is used in chord formation, and the **Melodic,** used in passages of melody in which harmonic relationships are not considered. This latter form is simpler and easier to read, as it generally requires fewer accidentals. The two forms of the chromatic scale are exactly alike in descending, differing only in the upward progression.

NOTE.—In Sol-fa the vowel of a note lowered a semitone is altered to ' a ' (pronounced ' aw ')—te becoming **ta,** lah becoming **la,** &c. The vowel of a note raised a semitone is altered to ' e '— **doh** becoming **de, ray** becoming **re,** &c. The flat of **soh** is not used, as it never occurs in any harmonic relationship. The note between **f** and **s** is, therefore, always called **fe.**

Ex. 56.
(*a*)
(Major)

C. HARMONIC CHROMATIC

d r a r ma m f fe s la l ta t d' t ta l la s fe f m ma r ra d

(Minor)

l₁ ta₁ t₁ d de r re m f fe s se l se s fe f m re r de d t₁ ta₁ l₁

(b)   C. MELODIC CHROMATIC

(c)   E. HARMONIC CHROMATIC

(Major)

(Minor)

(d)   E. MELODIC CHROMATIC

81. It is useful to remember which notes of the scale have only one letter name. In the Harmonic form these are the Tonic (1) and Dominant (5), and in the Melodic form the Mediant (3) and Leading-note (7), and *always* the Tonic and Dominant in descending.

A good aid to the memory is to keep in mind the first four odd numbers, and to think of them in pairs, 1 3 5 7 ; Harmonic 1–5, Melodic 3–7, and always 1–5 descending.

82. The Melodic Chromatic is rarely used in a minor key, as it only differs from the Minor Harmonic Chromatic in the second note—le instead of ta. The single notes ascending are the Supertonic (2) and Dominant (5).

The major and minor (old form) scales are survivals from the Church modes which were in use in medieval times. The following are those known as the **Authentic** modes. It will be noticed that the order of the tones and semitones (marked with a slur) varies in each case :

Ionian.

Dorian.

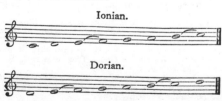

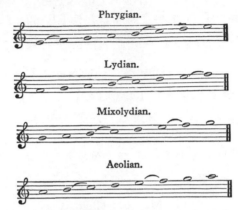

Phrygian.

Lydian.

Mixolydian.

Aeolian.

The major scale in present use is identical with the Ionian mode, and the various forms of the minor scale (see p. 32) are derived from the Aeolian mode. The Dorian mode has survived to a large extent in German chorales, e.g. 'Erschienen ist der herrliche Tag', and folk-songs, e.g. 'Wha wadna fecht for Charlie'.

Bach describes a Toccata and Fugue in D minor for organ as being in the Dorian mode.

The **Pentatonic**, or five-note scale, is probably the oldest scale. Its most usual form is like the modern diatonic major scale with the 4th and 7th degrees omitted.

Pentatonic.

(By regarding F♯ or G♭ as the tonic, the scale may be played on the black keys only of the pianoforte.) The hymn-tunes 'Selma' and 'Ballerma' and the song 'Ye banks and braes' are examples of melodies written in this scale. Other forms of the scale can be obtained by taking any of the other notes as the tonic. The air known as 'Ladie Cassilles Lilt' is an example with G as the tonic.

The **Whole-tone** scale has been employed by certain modern composers, chief among whom is Debussy.

Whole-tone scale.

As all seconds are major, all thirds major or diminished, and all fourths and fifths imperfect, it is obvious that the use of this scale is limited in its possibilities.

Note on Sol-fa notation.—A stroke is placed above or below a note to indicate the sound an octave higher or lower, e.g. d-d¹, s-s₁; the figure 2 indicating two octaves, e.g. l-l¹-l². For the Treble or Alto part any Doh between middle C and the B above, and for the Tenor or Bass part any Doh between middle B and the C below is unmarked, and is called the *Unmarked Doh*. The notes from Ray to Te have the same marking as the Doh below.

A change of key is shown by a note in small type called a *Bridge Note*, e.g. ˢd. This indicates that the singer is to sing the sound of the note Soh, at the same time calling it Doh, and continue accordingly.

CHAPTER 6

INTERVALS

83. THE difference between the pitch of two sounds is called an **Interval.** When the notes of an interval are sounded together, it is said to be **Harmonic**; when they are sounded in succession, it is called **Melodic.**

Ex. 57.   Harmonic.   Melodic.

84. The number of the interval is reckoned by counting the number of letter-names from one note to the other, the names of both sounds being included.

85. Sounds at the same pitch are said to be in **Unison.** Intervals between notes having adjacent letter-names (as A–B) are **Seconds,** as two letters are involved; intervals having three letter-names (as A–C) are **Thirds,** as three letters A–B–C are included.

86. If one or both of the notes is raised or lowered by a sharp, flat, &c., the number of the interval remains the same. For example, C–G and C–G♯ are both fifths, though one is a larger interval than the other. This difference of size apart from the number is called the **Quality** of the interval.

87. The quality of intervals is most easily calculated by regarding the lower note as the tonic of a major scale. Reckoning upwards from the tonic,

d–r   d–m   d–l   d–t   are called *Major,*
d–d   d–f   d–s   d–d¹   are called *Perfect*

(because, as will be seen later, Perfect intervals alone retain the same quality when inverted).

Ex. 58.
Maj. 6th.   Perf. 5th.   Maj. 3rd.   Perf. 4th.   Maj. 7th.   Perf. Unison.   Maj. 2nd.

88. Intervals may vary in quality by the inflexion of either the upper or the lower note. Thus:

(1) An interval which is one semitone less than a major one is termed **Minor.**

Ex. 59.   Maj.   Min.   Min.   Maj.   Min.   Min.

(2) An interval which is one semitone less than a Perfect or Minor one is termed **Diminished.** (Consequently a diminished interval is two semitones less than a major one.)

Ex. 60.

Maj. Min. Min. Dim. Dim. Dim. Perf. Dim. Dim. Dim. Dim.

(3) An interval which is one semitone greater than a Perfect or Major one is termed **Augmented.** (Consequently an augmented interval is two semitones greater than a minor one.)

Ex. 61.　　　　　Min. Maj. Maj. Aug. Aug. Aug.

89. Suppose the following is given: 'Add *above* the notes in Ex. 62 the intervals required.'

Ex. 62.　　　　(*a*)　　　(*b*)　　　(*c*)　　　(*d*)

Maj. 6th. Min. 3rd. Dim. 5th. Aug. 6th.

The method of working is as follows. First insert the note which gives the correct number of the interval regardless of its quality, and then modify it if necessary to obtain the quality required.

(*a*) A 6th above F is D, which we place above F. Taking F♯ as the tonic of a major scale, the sixth note of that scale is D♯. D♮ being one semitone lower, the interval as it stands is therefore a minor 6th, and the D will require to be raised a semitone to D♯ to make it major.

(*b*) The 3rd above B is D. D being the third note of the scale of B♭, the interval B♭–D is a major 3rd, and the D will require to be flattened a semitone to make it minor.

(*c*) The 5th above E is B. As B is the 5th note of the scale of E the interval E–B is perfect. The B will therefore require to be flattened a semitone to make the interval diminished.

(*d*) The 6th above A is F. The sixth note of the scale of A is F♯, therefore an augmented 6th above A will be a semitone above F♯, i.e. F×.

Ex. 63.　　　　(*a*)　　　(*b*)　　　(*c*)　　　(*d*)

Maj. 6th. Min. 3rd. Dim. 5th. Aug. 6th.

90. ' Add *below* the notes given in Ex. 64 the intervals required.'

Ex. 64.

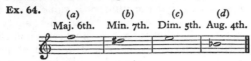

As before, first insert the note which will represent the correct number of the interval, regardless of its quality. Then take the major scale of the *lower* note to find the quality of the interval as it stands, after which raise or lower the *lower* note, if necessary, to the quality required.

(*a*) The 6th below F is A. The sixth note of the scale of the lower note A is F♯, therefore F♮ (the note given) is a minor 6th above A. To make the interval major the lower note will require to be lowered a semitone by a flat. F being the sixth note of the scale of A♭ major, the interval A♭–F is therefore a major 6th.

(*b*) The 7th below D is E. As D♯ is the seventh note of the scale of E, the interval E–D♯ is a major 7th. To make it minor the lower note E will require a sharp, thus lessening the interval by one semitone.

(*c*) The 5th below E is A. E being the fifth note of the scale of A, the interval is a perfect 5th as it stands. To make it diminished the lower note will therefore require to be raised a semitone by a sharp.

(*d*) The 4th below B is F. The fourth note of the scale of F is B♭, therefore the interval as it stands is a perfect 4th. To augment it, the lower note will require a flat.

Ex. 65.

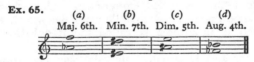

91. If it is required to calculate an interval in which the lower note is one not having a major key-signature, e.g. A♯ or F♭, the best method is to take the note minus the sharp or flat as the tonic, and first find out the quality of the interval without it, e.g.

(*a*) Taking F as the tonic of the scale, D is the sixth note, so that F–D is a major 6th. F♭–D is therefore an augmented 6th.

(*b*) B–D is a minor 3rd, therefore B♯–D is a diminished 3rd.

It must be remembered that the numerical value of an interval is decided by the alphabetical names. When the quality of the interval is altered, these alphabetical names must remain unchanged. For instance, in Ex. 63 (*d*) above, A–F×, if the upper note was written as G instead of F×, the interval would be changed from a 6th to a 7th, although the two notes represent the same sound.

In writing an interval above or below a given note, it is important to remember that it is the *added note alone* which is modified when necessary, the given note remaining unchanged.

92. The term 'augmented unison', applied to a chromatic semitone such as F–F♯, is obviously a misnomer, but it may be used for convenience, as also the term 'diminished octave', e.g. C♯–C¹.

93. There are therefore five qualities of intervals—Perfect, Major, Minor, Diminished, and Augmented. We can tabulate them as follows:

A Perfect interval (1, 4, 5, and 8) ⎱ is one in which the upper
A Major interval (2, 3, 6, and 7) ⎰ note belongs to the major scale of the lower note.

A Minor interval is one semitone less than a Major.

A Diminished interval is one semitone less than a Minor or a Perfect.

An Augmented interval is one semitone greater than a Major or a Perfect.

94. An interval on which the ear can dwell, without the desire for another to follow, is called **Consonant**. One which gives a desire for some other sound to follow is **Dissonant,** and the sound to which it progresses is called the **Resolution** of the dissonance.

95. Consonant and Dissonant intervals may be classified as follows:

CONSONANT		DISSONANT.
Perfect Consonant	*Imperfect Consonant*	
All Perfect intervals.	All major and minor 3rds and 6ths.	All Diminished and Augmented intervals, and all 2nds and 7ths.

To understand the difference in the nature of two such intervals as the dissonance C–G♯ and the consonance C–A♭, both of which have the same sound when played alone, requires a knowledge of

Harmony. The difference will be felt, however, when the harmony is completed by the addition of the note E in the first case, and E♭ in the second.

96. An interval not exceeding an octave is said to be a **Simple Interval**, one exceeding an octave a **Compound Interval**. For purposes of harmony, however, compound intervals are generally regarded as simple, a 10th being a 3rd, a 12th a 5th, &c.

Inversion of Intervals

97. Intervals may be inverted by reversing the position of the two notes, i.e. placing the lower above the higher, or vice versa. All intervals change their number on inversion. The number of the inversion of a simple interval may be found by subtracting from 9, e.g. a 3rd becomes a 6th, a 5th a 4th, &c. On inversion all intervals change their quality except the Perfect (see p. 37, Par. 87).

Major intervals become Minor.
Minor intervals become Major.
Diminished intervals become Augmented.
Augmented intervals become Diminished.

The Keys in which an Interval may occur

98. To find the keys in which a given interval may occur diatonically (i.e. when both notes belong to the Diatonic scale of that key), first find the number and quality of the interval given. Then find on which degrees of the major and minor scale the interval having that particular number and quality combined occurs. Regard the notes given as those degrees of the scale, and find the tonic.

Take for example the question:

In how many keys can the interval ♭ be found?

This being a major third, we proceed to find between which degrees of the major and minor scales a major third is found.

Ex. 66.

In a major scale the major thirds will be found to lie between the 1st and 3rd, the 4th and 6th, and the 5th and 7th. Now, taking the notes of the interval given, and giving them those numbers, it will be seen that Ab and C are the 1st and 3rd notes of the scale of Ab major, the 4th and 6th of the scale of Eb major, and the 5th and 7th of the scale of Db major.

In the same way, taking a minor scale (Harmonic),

Ex. 67.

the major thirds will be found between the 3rd and 5th, the 5th and 7th, and 6th and 8th degrees. Therefore Ab and C are the 3rd and 5th notes of the scale of F minor, the 5th and 7th of the scale of Db minor, and the 6th and 8th of the scale of C minor.

The interval Ab–C therefore belongs to the keys of Ab, Eb, and Db major, and F, Db, and C minor.

99. In how many keys can the interval ![interval notation] be found?

This being an augmented 4th, find between which degrees of the major and minor scale this particular interval is found.

The following scales show all the augmented 4ths to be found in the major and minor scales:

Ex. 68. (a)

(b)

It will be seen that the augmented 4th occurs once in the major scale, between the 4th and 7th degrees, and twice in the minor scale, between the 4th and 7th, and the 6th and 2nd, so that this interval belongs to three keys, one major and two minor.

Taking the notes of the interval given, and giving them the above numbers, we find that Bb and E are the 4th and 7th notes of the scale of F major, the 4th and 7th of F minor, and the 6th and 2nd of D minor.

100. By following the above method the keys of any given interval may be found. It must be remembered that in some cases the key is one not having a key-signature, e.g. the key of D♭ minor above, which, if it represented the key of the piece, would be written with the signature of C♯ minor, its enharmonic. It will often be found, however, that in the course of a piece of music a modulation is made to a key having more than seven sharps or flats, the scale of which will require one or more double sharps or flats. (See Fugue No. 3, Book I of Bach's *48 Preludes and Fugues*, where there is in bars 19–22 a modulation to the key of E♯ minor.)

101. It will be found helpful to study the following scales, in which are shown above *all* the diminished intervals, and below, *all* the augmented, their inversions:

Ex. 69. (*a*)

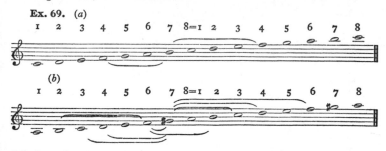

All the other intervals are perfect, major, or minor.

102. In some cases the interval given can be found only in the chromatic scale. This is called a **Chromatic Interval,** and in finding the keys to which it belongs, the **Harmonic** form of the chromatic scale must be used (see p. 34). As an example take the augmented 6th F–D♯. On examining the chromatic scale, two intervals of the augmented 6th will be found, one between the minor 2nd and major 7th from the tonic, and the other between the minor 6th and augmented 4th.

Ex. 70.

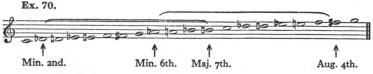

F and D♯ are therefore the minor 2nd and major 7th of the scale of E, and the minor 6th and augmented 4th of the scale of A. As the major and minor forms of the harmonic chromatic scale are

alike, the above interval belongs (chromatically) to four keys,
E major and minor, and A major and minor. If the interval given
is a diminished 3rd, the inversion of the augmented 6th, the same
process as above can be carried out by inverting the interval.

After the process of finding keys has become familiar, it may be
found sufficient to consider only the lower note of the interval given.
Take, for instance, the first example given above, the interval of the
major 3rd, Ab–C. We find that the major 3rd occurs on the 1st, 4th,
and 5th degrees of a major scale, therefore the Ab is the 1st, 4th, and
5th degree of the major scales of Ab, Eb, and Db respectively.

For the augmented 6th call the *lower* note, and for its inversion
the diminished 3rd the *upper* note, the minor 2nd and minor 6th
from the tonic of the scale.

CHAPTER 7

ORNAMENTS AND ABBREVIATIONS

103. Acciaccatura (Crushed note). This ornament is not found in music prior to about the year 1750. It is a very short note played before the principal note. The acciaccatura is played on the beat, and takes its time value from the principal note, which retains the accent. It is written as a quaver in small type, with a stroke through the stem and hook ♪

Ex. 71.

(a) *Adagio.* Played.

(b) *Allegro con brio.* BEETHOVEN. Played.

(c) *Adagio molto.* BEETHOVEN. Played.

(d) *Allegro.* BEETHOVEN. Played.

(e) *Allegro.* BEETHOVEN. Played.

[Double Acciaccatura—see Schleifer.]

(f) *Andante.* CHOPIN. Played.

In Ex. (f) it will be noticed that the acciaccatura takes its time value from the preceding note, and not from the principal note. This is because the pitch of the acciaccatura is the same as that of its principal note.

(g)   CHOPIN.   Played.

104. **Appoggiatura** (Leaning note). An auxiliary note placed before the principal note, from which it takes its time and accent. Since about the year 1800 the custom has been to write the appoggiatura exactly as played, but before that time it was written in small type, the idea evidently being to make the harmonic structure clearer to the eye. The old form may, however, be found in Beethoven's early works, and in most of the works of Schubert.

The following rules for the interpretation of the appoggiatura, by J. J. Quantz (1697–1773), a contemporary of J. S. Bach, are recommended:

(a) 'Appoggiature are found on a long note on the accented beat which follows a short one on an unaccented beat. One must hold the appoggiatura half the value of the principal note.'

Ex. 72. Written.   Played.

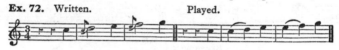

(b) 'If the appoggiatura belongs to a dotted note, the latter is divided in three parts, of which the appoggiatura takes two and the principal note only one, that is, the value of the dot.'

Written.   Played.

(c) 'When in a ⁶₄ or ⁶₈, two notes are tied together, and the first has a dot after it, as happens in the Gigues, one must hold the appoggiatura the whole value of the dotted note.'

Written.   Played.

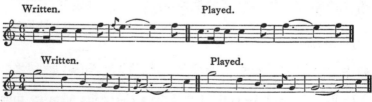

(d) 'When there is an appoggiatura to a note followed by a rest, you must give to the appoggiatura the whole time of the principal note, and to the latter the time of the rest.'

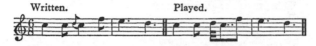

(*e*) 'Appoggiature between two notes of the same pitch—

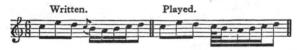

and an appoggiatura to a note of the shortest value used in the passage where it occurs, must be played very short.'

(*f*) 'An appoggiatura to a note forming a discord with the bass (2nd, 7th, augmented 4th, diminished 5th, &c.) must be played very short or else the discord will be changed into a concord and the harmony spoiled.'

105. **Arpeggio** (It. *Arpa*=Harp). The sounding of the notes of a chord in succession, either ascending or descending.

(*a*) The chord may be written as played—

Ex. 73.

the exact note values being given. In piano music the complete chord may be held by means of pedalling.

(*b*) The chord may have the sustained arpeggio effect indicated thus—

in which case the notes are played one after the other as rapidly as possible from the lowest upwards, all the notes, if practicable, being sustained during the value of the chord.

Ex. 74.

When the chord is divided between the two hands, and it is desired that the hands should begin the arpeggio together, the sign is divided, as at (*d*). When the notes are intended to be played one after the other from the lowest to the highest, the sign is unbroken, as at (*e*).

When the sign is written thus—

Ex. 75.

the order in which the notes are played is reversed—

106. Sometimes the arpeggio is combined with an acciaccatura or appoggiatura, in which case the latter is played before the note against which it is placed.

Ex. 76. Written. Played. Written. Played.
(a) (b)

107. **Mordent** ᴧᴡ (sometimes called the **Inverted** or **Lower Mordent**). An ornament consisting of the principal note, the note *below*, and the principal note, played as quickly as possible in the time of the principal note. The last note is the longest, and unless the speed of the music is very fast, receives the accent. In old music the note below in the scale is understood, but if the note of the scale is a full tone, and a semitone is required (as is generally the case in modern music), an accidental is placed below the sign,

ᴧᴡ ᴧᴡ ᴧᴡ
♯ ♮ × .

Ex. 77.

(a) *Andante con moto.* BACH. Played.

(b) *Allegro.* BACH. Played.

(c) *Allegretto moderato.* BACH. Played.

108. **Pralltriller** ᴧᴡ (a transient shake) may consist of the same number of notes as the Mordent (when it is sometimes called the **Upper Mordent**), viz. the principal note, the note *above*, and the principal note played as quickly as possible; or the reiteration

E

of the two notes may be continued, producing the effect of a short shake. The latter is only found in old music, and is written thus ⟋⟍.

Ex. 78.
(a) *Allegro.* Bach. Played.
(b) *Vivace.* Bach. Played.
(c) *Allegro moderato.* Bach. Played.
(d) *Allegro.* Bach. Played.

109. **Nachschlag** (After-note), expressed by a curved line ⌣, ⌣, or a stroke ▬. The Nachschlag is found in old music, and is a short note placed as a passing-note, or note of anticipation, between two harmony notes:

Ex. 79. (a) Written. Played. (b) Written. Played.

When the two harmony notes are of the same pitch the sign ∧ or ∨ is used to indicate that the note above or below is required:

Ex. 80. (a) Written. Played. (b) Written. Played.

110. **Schleifer** (Slide), expressed in old music by the sign ⟋⟍. This consists of a progression of two ascending diatonic notes leading scalewise to a harmony note. The time of the notes forming the slide is taken from the value of the following harmony note.

Ex. 81. BACH. Played.

In modern music it is either written as played or as a Double Acciaccatura.

111. **Shake,** or **Trill** (Italian, *Trillo*), indicated in old music by the sign *∿*, *∿*, *tr*, or *tr∿*, and in modern music by *tr* or *tr∿*, is the rapid and regular alternation of the note and the note of the scale above (unless otherwise indicated by an accidental placed over the sign; and when it occurs on the submediant of a minor key, in which case the flattened 7th is played to avoid the interval of an augmented 2nd):

Ex. 82. BACH. Played.

&c.

112. Generally speaking, in music composed before the year 1750 the shake should commence on the upper note, and in music composed since that date on the principal note, unless otherwise directed, either by the addition of short notes in small type, or by a variation in the shape of the sign.

113. The Shake generally ends with a Turn (see p. 54), which may or may not be indicated.

The following examples will give a general idea as to their interpretation, but, as in the case of most ornaments, much is left to the taste and discretion of the performer, especially with regard to old music:

Ex. 83.

(a) *Allegro.* BACH.

Played.

(b) *Allegro vivace.* BACH. Played.

Played.

(NOTE.—When the shake is on a dotted note followed by a note equal in value to the dot, as at *, the last note of the shake takes the place and time of the dot.)

(*l*) *Andante sostenuto.* CHOPIN. Played.

(*m*) *Allegretto.*   CHOPIN.

Played.

When a shake occurs on a short note in quick time it is generally played as a triplet (*n*).

(*n*) *Allegro.*   MOZART. Played.

114. **Chain of Shakes** (Italian, *Catena di Trilli*). This is a series of shakes on successive notes. The turn should be added only to the last shake, unless otherwise indicated.

Ex. 84.

Adagio un poco mosso.   BEETHOVEN.

Played.

115. The following signs to indicate the beginnings and endings of shakes are to be found in old music:

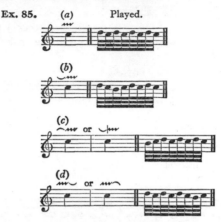

Ex. 85. (a) Played.

(b)

(c)

(d)

116. The **Turn** (Italian, *Gruppetto*) is indicated by the sign ∼ placed over or after the principal note or by writing in small type the notes to be played. These are—the note above, the principal note, the note below, and the principal note.

Ex. 86. Played.

117. In old music the note above and below in the scale should be played unless otherwise directed. In modern music the custom is to indicate the exact note required by an accidental placed above or below the sign:

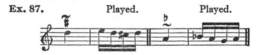

Ex. 87. Played. Played.

118. When, in a minor key, the turn occurs on the leading-note, the note below must be the major 6th of the scale, in order to avoid the interval of the augmented 2nd:

Ex. 88. Played.

119. When the principal note is preceded by a rest or by a staccato note, the turn generally commences on the principal note, and is written as a quintuplet:

Ex. 89.

120. When the turn is placed on or after a dotted note followed by a note of the same value as the dot but not of the same pitch as the principal note, and the dot and the following note both occupy the same beat or portion of a beat, the last note of the turn takes the place and time of the dot (in the case of a double-dotted note, both dots).

Ex. 90.

121. An **Inverted Turn** ꜱ (sometimes ꜱ ∼ or ᴗ) indicates that the order of the notes above and below the principal note is reversed, thus beginning with the note below instead of the note above:

Ex. 91.

122. When a turn is placed *over* a long note, or when it occurs in slow tempo, the last note is longer than the others:

Ex. 92. (*a*)   (*b*) *Adagio.*

123. When a turn is placed *after* a long note, the duration of the principal note should be as long as possible:

Ex. 93.

124. The following are a few examples of turns from the works of various composers :

Ex. 94.

(a) *Largo.*   C. P. E. Bach.   Played.

(b) *Allegro.*   Mozart.   Played.

(c) *Allegretto.*   Mozart   Played.

(d) *Adagio molto.*   Beethoven.   Played.

(e) *Allegro molto.*   Beethoven.   Played.

(f) *Adagio.*   Beethoven.   Played.

(g) *Allegro.*   Beethoven.   Played.

(h) *Allegro.*   Beethoven.   Played.

(i)   Weber.   Played.

ABBREVIATIONS

125. In order to save time and labour in writing, composers and copyists use signs to indicate that certain bars or groups of notes have to be repeated. The following are a few examples in common use:

Ex. 95. (a) (b) (c) (d) (e) (f) (g) (h) (i) (j) (k) (l) (m)

* It must be remembered that the two minims represent the time value of one minim only. They are written one after the other to show that they are played alternately and not together, as in the previous example.

(n) Written. *(o)*

Played.

126. **Tremolo** (Trem.) indicates that the notes must be reiterated as rapidly as possible:

Ex. 96. *Trem. Trem.*

127. In concerted music, where the performers are playing or singing from a single stave, and a rest of several bars occurs, it is usual to write across an empty bar the number of bars that are silent:

Ex. 97.

At the end of several bars rest, a *Cue* consisting of a few notes from another part is sometimes given in small type as a guide to the next entry.

128. The repetition of a single bar or more is sometimes indicated by the word **Bis** (meaning twice).

129. Dots placed before a double bar indicate that the music has to be repeated from the beginning or from a previous double bar with dots after it, e.g. :‖ Dots placed after a double bar indicate that the music following must be repeated from that point, e.g. ‖: :‖

130. If on repetition there is a change in the ending of the music, the words *1ma volta* (1st time) and *2da volta* (2nd time) are placed over the different endings. Sometimes only the figures 1 and 2 are used:

Ex. 98.

The bar marked 1 is omitted at the repetition, and that marked 2 played instead.

CHAPTER 8

CHORD FORMATION AND CADENCES

131. Two or more sounds of different pitch heard at the same time make what is called a **Chord.** The art of combining chords is called **Harmony.**

The most common form of chord consists of three notes, a fundamental note or **Root,** with a third and a fifth above it. A chord of this nature is called a **Triad.**

There are four kinds of Triad, formed in the following ways:
(1) The root, a major 3rd, and a perfect 5th above.

Ex. 99.

These are called **Major Triads**, as the 3rd is major.
(2) The root, a minor 3rd, and perfect 5th above.

Ex. 100.

These are called **Minor Triads**, as the 3rd is minor.
(3) The root, a minor 3rd, and diminished 5th above.

Ex. 101.

These are called **Diminished Triads,** as the 5th is diminished.
(4) The root, a major 3rd, and augmented 5th above.

Ex. 102.

These are called **Augmented Triads,** as the 5th is augmented.
132. On playing the above chords it will be noticed in the case of the major and minor triads that the mind does not desire some other chord to follow, whereas the diminished and augmented triads give a feeling of incompleteness, requiring something else to follow to satisfy the ear. The former are **Consonant,** and are called **Concords,** the latter being **Dissonant** and termed **Discords.** The chord to which a discord naturally moves is termed the **Resolution** of the dissonance.

Of these four kinds of triad, the two which are consonant—the major and the minor—are known as **Common Chords.** The two dissonant ones—the diminished and augmented—are called **Imperfect Triads.**

133. Triads may be formed on any degree of the major or minor scale by taking the note of the scale as the root and adding above it a 3rd and 5th. The triads thus formed will be seen to vary in their quality :

It will be noticed that the **Harmonic** form of the minor scale is used, this being the form used in chord formation (see p. 32).

134. If we add a third above the highest note of the triad on the dominant, that is, a seventh from the root, we shall find the intervals to be the same both in the major and minor keys, a major 3rd, perfect 5th, and minor 7th. If we add a 7th to any other of the triads, we shall find that on no other degree of the scale do we get that particular combination of intervals.

This chord, the intervals of which are peculiar to the Dominant of the major and minor keys, is known as the chord of the **Dominant Seventh :**

135. If we add a seventh to the triad on the leading-note of the minor scale we shall find a combination of intervals only to be found on this degree of the minor scale, and on no degree of the major scale—a minor 3rd, diminished 5th, and diminished 7th. This is called the chord of the **Diminished Seventh :**

136. When the root of a chord is in the bass (the bass being the lowest note of any chord at whatever pitch it may occur) the chord is said to be in **Root Position**.   When the root is removed from the bass and placed in an upper part, leaving the third of the chord as the bass note, the chord is said to be in its **First Inversion**:

Ex. 106.   Root position.   1st Inversion.

137. When the fifth of the chord is placed as the bass note, the chord is in its **Second Inversion**:

Ex. 107.   Root position.   2nd Inversion.

138. The chords of the 7th having four notes have therefore four positions, the root position and three inversions:

Ex. 108.   Dominant 7th.   Diminished 7th.

In the chord of the diminished 7th, when the notes are placed close together as in Ex. 108*, the interval between each note consists of three semitones, therefore when the chord is heard alone there are no real inversions, the difference being one of notation only.   The mental effect, however, is felt in relation to the prevailing key.   Compare the following examples, in which (*a*) is the root position of the diminished 7th in G minor, and (*b*) the first inversion of the diminished 7th in E minor, with E♭ enharmonically changed to D♯:

Ex. 109.   (*a*)   (*b*)

139. As will be seen in the above examples the distribution of the *upper* notes does not affect the nature of the chord.   So long as the root, or the 3rd, or the 5th, or the 7th of the chord is in the lowest part, the chord is respectively in the root position, first, second, or third inversion.

140. In writing music for four voices or instruments, it follows that in using triads, which have three notes only, one of the notes

must be used in two of the parts. This is called **Doubling** a note. As a general rule, in writing isolated triads, the following are the best notes to double.

141. Major and Minor Common chords. Root position and second inversion—double the bass note. First inversion—place either the root or the 5th in the treble and double that:

Ex. 110. (*a*) Root position.

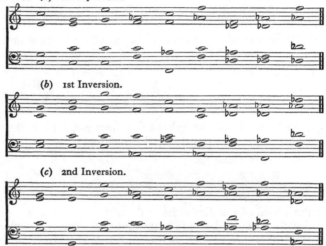

(*b*) 1st Inversion.

(*c*) 2nd Inversion.

142. Diminished Triads. These are rarely used in their root position and second inversion. They are very often used in the first inversion, and are then classed as consonant, as both the upper notes, though dissonant with each other (augmented 4th or diminished 5th), are consonant with the bass note (minor 3rd and major 6th).

In root position the best note to double is the third, in first inversion the bass note, in second inversion either the third or fifth of the chord. The leading-note should never be doubled:

Ex. 111.

Those in brackets occur but rarely.

143. **Augmented Triads.** These consist of two major thirds (four semitones) one above the other. When the lowest note is placed at the top we again get two intervals of four semitones each:

Ex. 112.

The same result is produced when the next position is taken:

Ex. 113.

All forms of the augmented triad are thus identical so far as the number of semitones between their notes is concerned, however these may be placed, and whatever enharmonic changes are made. In a sense, therefore, this chord has no inversions, yet the mental effect of Ex. 114 (*a*), which is the original position of the augmented triad of D, the mediant of B minor, is different from that of (*b*), which is the first inversion of the augmented triad of B♭, the mediant of G minor, both resolving on the submediant chord. If the examples below are played this will be realized:

Ex. 114.   (*a*)   (*b*)

The best notes to double are either the root or third of the chord:

Ex. 115.

144. Care should be taken to arrange the notes of a chord so that they are well balanced. The notes should be as far as possible equidistant from each other. An interval greater than an octave may appear between the tenor and bass, but rarely between the tenor and alto or alto and treble. As a rule the lower the pitch of the notes, the greater should be the interval between them, and vice versa.

145. **To describe a given chord** it is necessary first to rearrange the notes so that they form a series of thirds one above the other. The lowest note is then the root, and the nature of the chord will be found by calculating the intervals from the root to the notes of the chord. Suppose we are required to describe the following chords:

Ex. 116.   (a)   (b)   (c)   (d)   (e)   (f)

The following gives the above chords in their root positions, and without doubling in the triads:

   (a)   (b)   (c)   (d)   (e)   (f)

(a) Root B♭ with major 3rd and perfect 5th. The 3rd is in the bass, so it is the first inversion of the major common chord of B♭. (b) Root C, with minor 3rd and perfect 5th. The 5th is in the bass, so it is the second inversion of the common chord of C minor. (c) Root A with major 3rd, perfect 5th, and minor 7th, therefore a dominant 7th, and the 3rd being in the bass, in its first inversion. (d) Root F, with major 3rd and augmented 5th. The 3rd is in the bass so it is the first inversion of the augmented triad on F. (e) Root E, with minor 3rd, diminished 5th, and diminished 7th, therefore it is the chord of the diminished 7th. The 7th being in the bass, the chord is in its third inversion. (f) Root A, with minor 3rd and diminished 5th. The 3rd being in the bass, the chord is the first inversion of the diminished triad on A.

146. **To determine the keys** in which a given chord may be found, the same method will be applied as that given in Chap. 6 with regard to intervals. Suppose we are required to state in which keys the following chords may be found:

Ex. 117.   (a)   (b)   (c)

First proceed as above to find the root and nature of the chord.

(a) On reducing the chord to thirds, A♭–C–E♭, we find it to be the major common chord of A♭ in its first inversion. Referring to the triads of the major and minor scales as given on p. 60, we find that there is a major common chord on the 1st, 4th, and 5th degrees of the major scale, and on the 5th and 6th degrees of the minor scale. A♭ will therefore be the 1st degree of the scale of A♭, the 4th of E♭, and the 5th of D♭ major; the 5th of D♭, and the 6th of C minor. (b) Reducing the chord to thirds we find the chord to be E–G–B♭, a diminished triad, in its first inversion. Again referring to the scales on p. 60, we find that there is one diminished 5th chord in the major scale, on the 7th degree, and two in the minor scale, on the 2nd and 7th degrees. The root E will then be the 7th degree of the scale of F major, the 2nd of D minor, and the 7th of F minor. (c) A 2nd inversion of the chord of the dominant 7th of which the root is B. This chord occurs only on the dominant (5th degree) of both major and minor scales, so B is the dominant of the scales of E major and E minor.

CADENCES

147. On listening to music, we notice that there is an onward movement, endowing it with life by bringing the various groups of ideas into close relationship. This movement is called **Rhythm**. The term rhythm is often applied to the grouping of strong and weak beats, e.g. two or three pulse rhythm. Also to the grouping of notes of different values :

148. We notice also that in the movement are certain points of rest or repose, which occur more or less regularly, and to a greater or less degree. In melodies the points of rest are generally recognized by the rise and fall of the sounds, or by the prominence of certain sounds due to their greater length; in harmony by certain chord progressions called **Cadences** (Cadence = a close). They may be likened to punctuation in language. A section of music terminating with a cadence is called a **Rhythmic Period**.

149. In music there are in common use four kinds of cadence, two which give a feeling of finality and two of semi-finality.

(1) **Perfect** (also called **Authentic,** or **Full Close**), corresponding to the full stop or period in language. This is formed by the Tonic Chord preceded by dominant harmony, giving a complete sense of finality :

Ex. 118.

The Roman numeral below each chord in these and the following examples denotes the scale note which is the root. I implies the tonic chord; II supertonic, &c.; ⁷V means the dominant 7th.

(2) **Plagal.** This is a full close similar in effect to the perfect, in which the tonic chord is preceded by the subdominant chord:

(The Plagal is sometimes called the 'Amen' cadence, as it is generally used for the harmony of the 'Amen' after the final perfect cadence of a hymn-tune.)

(3) **Imperfect,** or **Half-close,** which may be said to correspond to a comma, semicolon, or colon. This cadence most usually ends on the dominant chord, preceded by any other chord. It terminates an incomplete statement, leading the mind forward to a completion of the statement:

(4) **Interrupted,** or **Deceptive Cadence,** in which dominant harmony, instead of progressing to the expected tonic, moves to some other chord, usually the submediant. This cadence may be likened to an exclamation mark, or note of interrogation:

150. In a minor key the perfect and plagal cadences often end with the chord of the tonic *major*. When in a minor key the final chord is made major by raising the third a semitone, it is called the *Tierce de Picardie* (Tierce = third):

Ex. 119.

151. When one or both of the cadence chords is in an inverted position, the cadence is called *Inverted*:

Ex. 120.

Inversions of chords are denoted by the addition of a letter to the root-number—*b* = 1st inversion, *c* = 2nd inversion, &c.

CHAPTER 9

MUSICAL TERMS

The following lists of Italian terms have been graded to some extent in order of difficulty, so as to meet the varying needs of students at different stages of progress. The German terms (par. 158-9) have been similarly graded, while the General terms (par. 161) are intended to form as complete an index as is possible in a small book of this nature.

152 ITALIAN. SECTION I

A, in, to.

Accelerando, gradually faster.

Adagio, slow.

Adagietto, rather slow.

Adagissimo, very slow.

Allargando, broadening.

Allegretto, rather merry and lively.

Allegro, merry and lively.

Andante, at a moderate pace.

Andantino, not so slow as *Andante*.

Capo, the beginning.

Crescendo, ⎯⎯ gradually louder.

Da, from. [ning.

Da capo (*D.C.*), from the begin-

Dal, from the, by the.

Dal Segno (*D.S.*), from the sign 𝄋.

Decrescendo, ⎯⎯ gradually softer.

Di, of, with, for.

Diminuendo, ⎯⎯ gradually softer.

Due, two.

Forte, *f*, loud.

Fortissimo, *ff*, very loud.

Forza, force, power.

Forzando ⎰ *fz* ⎰ forced, with strong
Forzato ⎱   ⎱ emphasis.

Grave, slow and solemn.

Largo, slow, broad.

Larghetto, rather slow.

Legato ⎯⎯, smooth and connected.

Lento, slow.

Loco, place. The passage to be played as written.

Mezzo, half.

Mezzo forte, *mf*, moderately loud.

Mezzo piano, *mp*, moderately soft.

Moderato, at a moderate pace.

Piano, *p*, soft.

Pianissimo, *pp*, very soft.

Poco, little.

Poco a poco, little by little.

Presto, quickly.

Prestissimo, very quickly.

Quattro, four.

Rallentando, gradually slower.

Ritardando, gradually slower.

Tre, three.

Un ⎱
Una ⎰ a, an, one.
Uno ⎰

153 SECTION II

Affretando, hurrying the pace.

Agitato, agitated.

Amabile, tender, amiable.

Amore, love, ardour.

Amoroso, in a tender style.

Anima, soul, feeling.

Animo, spirit, boldness.

Animato, animated.

A piacere, at pleasure.

Appassionato, passionately.

Arco, bow.

A tempo, in strict speed.

Attacca, go on immediately.

Brio, fire, vigour.

Calando, softer and slower by degrees.

Cantabile, in a singing style.
Con, with.
Con espressione, with expression.
Con moto, with motion.
Corda, a string.
Destra, right.
Dolce, sweetly, gently.
Espressione, expression.
Fine, end.
Fuoco, fire, energy.
Giusto, exact, just, strict.
Gravemente, with gravity.
Gusto, taste, expression.
In tempo, in time.
Largamente, in a broad style.
Lunga pausa, a long pause.
Maestoso, majestic, dignified.
Marcato, marked, accented.
Meno, less.
Mesto, sad.
Mestoso, sadly.
Mezza voce, half the power of the voice.

Mezzo staccato, a little detached.
Molto, much.
Morendo, dying away.
Mosso ⎱ motion, movement.
Moto ⎰
Ottava, octave or eighth.
Pausa, rest, pause, stop.
Più, more.
Prima (1ma) *volta*, first time.
Ritenuto, slower at once.
Seconda, second.
Seconda (2da) *volta*, second time.
Segno, a sign '𝄋'.
Simile, like, similarly.
Tempo, speed.
Tempo primo, the speed as at first.
Tenerezza, tenderness, delicacy.
Tenuto, held on, sustained.
Tre corde, three strings, release the soft pedal of pianoforte.
Una corda, one string, depress soft pedal of pianoforte.
Vivace, with life and energy.

154 SECTION III

A battuta, strictly in time.
A cappella, see p. 16.
Affettuoso, tender, affectionate.
Al ⎱ to the, in the style of.
Alla ⎰
Alla breve, see p. 16.
Amarevole, bitterly.
Amorevole, lovingly.
Appenato, grieved, afflicted.
Assai, very.
Barcarola, boat song.
Ben ⎱ well, good.
Bene ⎰
Breve, short.
Brillante, sparkling, brilliant.
Brioso, fiery, lively.
Calcando, pressing forward.
Calmato, with calmness.
Cantando, in the singing style.
Cantilena, the principal melody.
Cappella, church.

Cogli ⎫
Col ⎬ with the.
Colla ⎭
Colla parte, with the solo part.
Colla voce, with the voice part.
Con dolore ⎱ with grief and
Con duolo ⎰ pathos.
Con energia, with energy.
Con forza, with force.
Con fuoco, with fire.
Con grazia, with grace.
Con gusto, with taste.
Con sordino, with mute.
Con sordini (with mutes), release sustaining (damper) pedal.
Con spirito, with spirit and energy.
Con tenerezza, with tenderness.
Dolente, sorrowful.
Dolore, sorrow, grief.
Doloroso, sorrowfully, sadly.

Doppio, double.

Doppio tempo, double speed, twice [as fast.

Dritta \
Dritto } right.

Duolo, grief, sorrow.

E \
Ed } and.

Energia, energy, force.

Espressivo, expressive.

Facile, easy.

Feroce, fierce, bold.

Fieramente, fiercely, boldly.

Furioso, furious, vehement.

Giocoso, gaily, merrily.

Giojoso, joyous, merry.

Gran pausa (*G.P.*), a rest for all performers.

Grazia, grace, elegance.

Grazioso, graceful, elegant.

Gruppetto, a turn.

I \
Il } the.

Incalzando, quicker and louder.

Istesso, the same.

La \
Le } the. \
Lo /

Legatissimo, very smooth.

Leggieramente, lightly, delicately.

Leggiero, light, delicate.

L'istesso, the same.

L'istesso tempo, continue in the same speed.

Lusingando, soothing, coaxing.

Ma, but.

Mancando, dying away.

Mano, the hand.

Mano destra \
Mano dritta } (*M.D.*), the right hand.

Mano sinistra (*M.S.*), the left [hand.

Marcia, a march.

Martellato, hammered.

Marziale, in the style of a march.

Mezzo soprano, low soprano [voice.

Non, not, no.

Non troppo, not too much.

Ottava alta, an octave higher.

Ottava bassa, an octave lower.

Parte, part.

Passionato, passionate, with fervour.

Pausa generale, a rest for all performers.

Perdendosi, dying away.

Pesante, heavy, ponderous.

Piacere, pleasure, fancy.

Piacevole, pleasing, agreeable.

Piangevole, plaintively, dolefully.

Pizzicato, the strings to be plucked by the fingers.

Quasi, like, almost.

Rinforzando, reinforced, strengthened, with energy and emphasis.

Rubato, robbed, not in strict time.

Scemando, decreasing in tone.

Scherzando, playful, lively.

Scherzo, play, sport, jest.

Sempre, always, continually.

Senza, without.

Senza sordini (without mutes), depress sustaining (damper) pedal.

Sforza \
Sforzando } *sf* { with force and energy.

Smorzando, extinguished, gradually dying away.

Soave, sweetly, gently.

Sordino, a mute, a device to deaden the vibrations of instruments.

Sostenuto, sustaining the tone.

Sotto, under, below.

Sotto voce, softly, in an undertone.

Stringendo, pressing onwards.

Subito, at once, immediately.

Tanto, so much, as much.

Tempo comodo, convenient speed.

Tempo giusto, in strict speed.

Tempo rubato, not in strict speed.

Teneramente, tenderly.

Tosto, quick, rapid.

Tranquillo, calm, quiet.

Troppo, too much.

Un poco, a little.
Veloce, swiftly, rapidly.
Velocissimo, very rapidly.
Vigoroso, vigorous, energetic.
Vivo, lively, brisk.

Voce, the voice.
Volta, time.
Volti, turn, turn over.
Volti subito (V.S.), turn over quickly.

155   Section IV

Ardito, bold.
Canto, song, air.
Capriccio, in a capricious, free [style.
Celere, quick, rapid.
Coda, the end or tailpiece.
Codetta, short coda.
Come, as, like, the same as.
Come prima, as at first.
Come sopra, as above, as before.
Decisione, decision, firmness.
Del, of the.
Deliberato, deliberately.
Delicato, delicately.
Desto, sprightly, brisk.
Di grado, by degrees.
Diluendo, fading away.
Di molto, very much.
Elegante, elegant, graceful.
Estinguendo, becoming extinct.
Fantasia, fancy, imagination.
Ferma }
Fermato } firm.
Fermata, a pause.
Foco, fire, ardour.
Glissando, in a gliding manner.
Grado, a step, a degree.
Grandioso, noble, lofty.
Grosso, large, great.
Imperioso, imperious, pompous.
Impetuoso, impetuous.
Lacrimoso }
Lagnevole } sadly, doleful.
Lagrimoso }
Lamentoso, lamentable, mournful.
Languendo, languishing, feeble.
Maggiore, major.
Melodioso, melodious.
Minore, minor.   [ner.
Parlante, in a declamatory man-

Patetica, pathetic.
Per, for, by, through.
Placido, tranquil, calm.
Poi, then, after.
Poi a poi, by degrees.
Pomposo, pompous, stately.
Ponderoso, ponderously, heavily.
Preciso, precise, exact.
Pronto, quickly, promptly.
Questo, this.
Rapido, rapid.
Religioso, religiously, in a devout manner.
Resoluto }
Risoluto } resolutely, boldly.
Rigore, rigour, strictness.
Rigoroso, rigorous, strict.
Risvegliato, animated.
Roccoco, old fashioned.
Rustico, rustic, rural.
Scioltamente, with freedom, agility.
Sciolto, free, light.
Secco, dry, unornamented, coldly.
Segue, follows.
Semplice, simple, plain.
Semplicemente, simply.
Sensibile, with feeling.
Serioso, seriously, gravely.
Sin al fine, to the end.
Sin' }
Sino } to, as far as, until.
Slargando }
Slentando } gradually slower.
Sonoro, sonorous, full-toned.
Sopra, above, over.
Soprano, the highest female voice.
Sorda, muffled, veiled tone.

Spianato, smooth, even.
Spirito, spirit, life, energy.
Spiritoso, lively, animated.
Strepitoso, noisy, boisterous.
Suave, sweet, mild.
Sul ⎫
Sull' ⎬ on, upon the.
Sulla ⎭
Sulponticello, play near the bridge.
Svegliato, brisk, sprightly.

Tace ⎫
Taci ⎬ be silent.
Tacet (Lat.) ⎭
Tema, a theme or melody.
Tempestoso, stormy, boisterous.
Tempo ordinario, ordinary, moderate time.
Tenero, tenderly, delicately.
Volante ⎫
Volata ⎬ in a flying manner.

156   Section V

Animoso, lively, bold.
Comodo, at an easy pace.
Devoto, devout.
Di bravura, in a florid brilliant style.
Di peso ⎫
Di posta ⎬ at once.
Elevato, elevated, sublime.
E poi, and then.
Fantastico, whimsical, capricious.
Fin a qui, to this place.
Fuga, a flight (see *Fugue*, p. 82).
Generoso, nobly.
Gentilmente, gently, gracefully.
Inconsolato, in a mournful style.
Indeciso, undecided.
Mobile, free, variable.
Negli ⎫
Nel ⎬ in the, at the.
Nello ⎭
Nobilmente, nobly, grandly.
Ossia, or, or else, otherwise.

Ostinato, continuous, unceasing.
Pochetto, a little.
Quieto, quiet, calm.
Raddolcente, softer by degrees.
Replica, reply, repetition.
Se, if, in case, as, so.
Spiccatamente ⎫ with springing
Spiccato ⎬ bow.
Stabile, firm.
Stretto, quicker (also see p. 88).
Tasto solo, the bass part alone, without harmony.
Timoroso, with hesitation.
Tostamente, quickly, rapidly.
Tutta forza, as loud as possible.
Un pochino, a very little.
Violento, violent, vehement.
Vistamente ⎫
Vitamente ⎬ quickly, swiftly.
Vivacetto, rather lively.
Vivacissimo, very lively.

157   Less Usual Italian Terms

Ancora, again, yet.
Aperto, open.
Calore, warmth, fire.
Che, than, which.
Chiara ⎫
Chiaro ⎬ clear, pure.
Con alcuna licenza, with a little licence.
Continuo, continued.
Corona, a pause ⌒.
Corretto, correct.
Da lontano, from a distance.

Divoto, devoutly.
Empito, impetuously.
Enfasi, emphasis.
Enunciato, enunciated.
Eroica, heroic.
Falotico, fantastical.
Fantoso, proud, stately.
Festoso, merry, gay.
Flebile, doleful, sad.
Freddo, cold, frigid.
Fretta, accelerating the time.
Furore, fury, passion.

Gagliardo, spirited, vigorous.
Gaia ⎱ gay, merry.
Gaio ⎰
Garbato, graceful.
Garbo, simplicity, grace.
Gaudioso, merry, joyful.
Giulivo, cheerful, gay.
Indegnato, angrily, furiously.
Infervorato, fervent, impassioned.
Innocenza, simplicity.
Lauda, laud, praise.
Lesto, quick, lively.   [strained.
Negligente, negligent, uncon-
Nettamente, neatly, clearly.
O, or, as, either.
Obbligato, indispensable, cannot be omitted.
Od, or, either.
Ordinario, ordinary, usual.
Pezzo, a piece of music.
Piangendo, plaintively.
Piena, full.
Pietà, pity, tenderness.
Portato, sustained, drawn out.
Posato, quietly, steadily.
Precipitando, hurrying.
Punta, the point.
Quasi campanella, like a bell.
Quasi niente, barely audible.
Rattenuto, holding back the time.
Ravvivando, reviving.   [ing-
Respiro, taking breath in sing-

Ripresa, a repeat.
Sciolo, arrogant.
Senza misura, without measure, not in strict time.
Sentito, with feeling.
Slancio, dash, impetuosity.
Smaniato, furious, frantic.
Soggetto, subject, theme.
Sonabile, sounding, resonant.
Sospiroso, sighing, doleful.
Spiccato, separated, detached.
Spronato, spurred.
Stentando, delayed, retarding.
Stentato, hard, loud, forced.
Stesso, the same.
Stinguendo, dying away.
Stiracchiato, retarding the time.
Strascicando, dragging the time.
Stravagante, odd, fantastic.
Svelto, free, light.

Tardamente, slowly.
Tedesca ⎱ German; *Alla Tedesca*,
Tedesco ⎰ in the German style.
Tepidità, coldness, indifference.
Turca, Turkish.
Tutte le corde, with all the strings; = *tre corde*.

Uguale, equal, similar.

Va, go on.
Vellutato, velvety, smooth.
Vezzoso, graceful, tender.

Abendlied, evening song.
Andächtig, devoutly.
Auf, on, upon, in, at.
Aus, from, out of.
Aus der Ferne, from the distance.
B, B♭ in English notation.
Betont, accented.
Bewegt, moved, agitated.
Breit, broad.
Clavier, keys of Piano or Organ.
Das, the.
Dem, to the.

Der ⎱ the.
Die ⎰
Dur, major.
Drei, three.
Ein ⎱ a, an, one.
Eine ⎰
Einfach, simple, plain.
Ernst, earnest, grave.
Erst, first.
Etwas, somewhat.
Ferne, distance.
Fest, feast or festival.

Feste }
Festigkeit } firmness, steadiness.
Festiglich, firmly.
Feuer, fire, ardour.
Frei, free, unrestrained.
Freude, joy.
Frisch, fresh, lively, vigorous.
Fröhlich, joyous.
Fuge, a fugue.
Gebunden, bound, slurred.
Gewichtig, heavy, weighty.
Glocke, a bell.
Glockenspiel, chimes.
Gross, great, large, major.
H, B in English notation.
Hastig, hasty, quick.
Heftig, vehement, impetuous.
Hoch, high.
Hohen, high, upper.
Hurtig, quickly.
Immer, always.
Klein, small, minor.
Kurz, short, detached.
Langsam, slowly.
Laut, loud.
Lebhaft, lively, vivacious.
Leicht, light, facile.
Leise, soft, gentle.
Liebeslied, love-song.
Lieblich, sweet, lovely.
Lied, song, air, ballad.
Lied ohne Worte, song without
Link, left.   [words.
Lustig, merrily, gaily.
Mässig, moderate.
Mit, with, by.
Moll, minor.
Morgengesang }
Morgenlied } morning-song.
Nach und nach, little by little.
Nicht, not.
Noch, still, yet.
Ober, upper, higher, above.

Oder, or, or else.
Ohne, without.
Präludium, introduction, prelude.
Rasch, fast.
Recht, right.
Rein, pure, clear.
Ruhig, quiet, soft.
Sanft, soft.
Scharf, sharp, acute.
Scherzlich, merrily, playfully.
Schnell, quickly, rapidly.
Schneller, quicker, faster.
Schwer, heavily, ponderously.
Sehr, very, much.
Singweise, melody, tune.
So, as, in this manner.
Stark, strong, loud, vigorous.
Still, calmly, quietly.
Stück, piece, air, tune.
Stückchen, little air or tune.
Süss, sweetly.
Tanz, dance.
Tief, deep, low.
Tiefer, deeper, lower.
Trauermarsch, funeral march.
Traurig, heavily, sadly.
Triumphlied, triumphal song.
Über, over.
Und, and.
Viel, much.
Vier, four.
Volkslied, folk-song or popular air.
Voll, full.
Voller, fuller.
Von, by, of, from, on.
Vorspiel, prelude.
Wenig, little.
Werk, work, movement.
Wie, as, as if.
Wort, word.
Zierlich, graceful.
Zu, to, at, by, for, in.
Zwei, two.

159 LESS USUAL GERMAN TERMS

Allmählich, gradually, by degrees.
Andacht, devotion.

Anfang, the beginning.
Aufgeweckt, brisk, lively.

Aufhalten, to retard.
Ausdruck, expression.
Ausdrucksvoll, with expression.
Aushalten, sustain.
Äusserst, extremely.
Bebung, shaking, oscillation.
Becken, cymbals.
Bedeutend, considerably.
Belebend, lively.
Bindung, tie, or bind (see p. 10).
Bogen, bow.
Bratsche, viola (see p. 90).
Dämpfer, mute.
Doch, but.
Doppel, double.
Doppelt so, twice as.
Drängend, hurrying.
Dreist, bold.
Drohend, threateningly.
Eilen, to hurry.
Einige, some, any.
Einschlafen, to die away.
Empfindung, emotion.
Entschieden, decided.
Entschlafen, to die away.
Erhaben, elevated, exalted.
Ermunterung, animation.
Ersterben, to die away.
Erweckung, animation.
Feierlich, solemn.
Fertig, quick, nimble.
Feurig, impetuously.
Fliessend, flowing, smooth.
Flüchtig, lightly, fleetly.
Gang, pace or speed.
Ganz, whole, very.
Gedehnt, sustained.
Gefällig, pleasingly, agreeably.
Gefühl, feeling, expression.
Gehalten, held, sustained.
Gehend, moving easily.
Geistreich⎫ spirited.
Geistvoll ⎭
Gelassen, calmly, quietly.
Geläufig, easy, fluent.
Gelinde, softly, gently.
Gemächlich ⎫ softly, slowly.
Gemachsam ⎭

Gemählich, by degrees.
Gemüt, soul.
Gemütlich, agreeable, expressive.
Gesang, song, melody.
Geschwind, quick, rapid.
Gestossen, short (*staccato*).
Geteilt, divided.
Gewöhnlich, ordinary.
Gezogen, sustained.
Gunst, grace, tenderness.
Hauptzeitmass, original speed.
Heiss, hot, ardent.
Heldenlied, heroic song.
Hervortretend, prominent.
Herzlich, tenderly.
Hochmut, dignity, loftiness.
Höflich, in a pleasing and graceful
Hold, agreeable, graceful. [style.
Innig, inward, heartfelt.
Kammer, chamber.
Kammermusik, chamber-music.
Keckheit, boldness, vigour.
Klang, sound, tune.
Klar, clear, bright.
Kraft, vigour, energy.
Kräftig, vigorously.
Kreuz, a sharp.
Landlied, rustic song.
Leben, life, vivacity.
Lebewohl, farewell.
Leidenschaftlich, passionately.
Leiter, leader.
Lobgesang, hymn of praise.
Markirt, marked.
Möglich, possible.
Munter, lively, sprightly.
Nachdruck, energy, emphasis.
Nachschlag, after-note (see p. 50).
Nachspiel, concluding piece.
Naiv, simple, artless.
Nett, neatly, clearly, plainly.
Pauke, kettle-drum.
Posaune, trombone.
Pult, desk.
Punkt, a dot, a point.
Saite, string.
Sanftheit, softness, gentleness.
Sänftig, soft, gentle.

Sang, song.
Satz, musical passage or subject.
Schäferlied, pastoral song.
Schleppend, dragging.
Schmelzend, dying away.
Schmerz, grief, sorrow.
Schmerzlich, in a dolorous man-
Schwach, soft. [ner.
Schwächer, softer, fainter.
Schwermütig, in a pensive melan-
choly manner.
Schwung, swing.
Sehnsucht, desire, longing.
Singstück, air, melody.
Ständchen, a serenade.
Standhaft, steadily, firmly.
Steg, bridge (stringed instru-
Stets, always. [ment).
Stimme, the voice, sound, part.
Streng, strict, rigid.
Stufe, step, degree.

Stürmisch, impetuously.
Takt, time, beat, bar.
Trommel, drum.
Übung, an exercise, study.
Veränderungen, variations.
Verhallend, dying away.
Verweilend, retarding the time.
Vorher, before.
Vorig, previous.
Wehmut
Wehmutig } melancholy.
Wehmutigkeit
Weich, soft, minor.
Wiederholung, repetition.
Wütend, furiously.
Zart } tenderly, softly.
Zärtlich
Zeitmass, speed.
Ziemlich, moderately.
Zögernd, retarding.
Zurückhaltend, holding back.

160   FRENCH TERMS

Abandon(avec), without restraint.
Agréments, graces, embellish-
ments.
À la chasse, in the hunting style.
Anche, reed.
Animé, animated.
Archet, bow, fiddle-stick.
Assez, rather.
Au, to the, at the, in the.
Avec, with.
Blanche, white note, minim.
Cédez, hold back.
Chaleur, warmth, ardour.
Chanterelle, the E string of a
violin.
Chasse, in the hunting style.
Clavecin, a harpsichord.
Clavier, a keyboard.
Clé, clef.
Clef, key.
Corde, string.
Croche, quaver.
Décidé, with decision.
Décisif, decisive, clear, firm.

De plus en plus vite, more and
more quickly.
Deux, two.
Dièse, a sharp.
Doigt, finger.
Double croche, semiqua er.
Doucement, softly, gently.
Douleur, grief, sorrow.
Doux, sweet, soft.
Droite, right.
Éclatant, loud, in a noisy manner.
École, school or method of in-
struction.
Égal, equal, even.
Emérillonné, sprightly.
Emporté, passionate.
Empressé, in haste.
En dehors, to stand out promi-
nently.
Enjoué, cheerful, gay.
En pressant, hurrying on.
Ensemble, together.
En se perdant, losing itself.
Eveillé, lively.

Expressif, expressively.
Facile, easy.
Fanfare, a flourish of trumpets, a trumpet tune.
Faux, false.
Fois, time.
Folâtre, playful.
Fonds, foundation stops (Organ).
Funèbre, funereal, mournful.
Fureur, fury, rage.
Gai, gay, merry.
Gamme, the gamut, or scale.
Gauche, left.
Haut, high, acute, shrill.
Hautbois, oboe.
Hautement, haughtily, dignified.
Jeu, style of playing an instrument, Organ stop.
Joie, delight, gladness.
La
Le } the.
Les
Laissez vibrer, allow (the note) to vibrate.
Léger, light, nimble.
Lent, slow. [bind.
Liaison, smoothness, a tie or
Lié, smoothly, tied.
Lointain, distant.
Lourdement, heavily.
Louré, a species of bowing.
Main, hand.
Main droite, the right hand.
Main gauche, the left hand.
Marqué, marked.
Martelé, hammered.
Même, the same. [tempo.
Même mouvement, in the same
Mesure, measure or bar.
Modéré, moderate.
Moins, less.
Molle, soft, mellow.
Mouvement, motion, movement.
Naïf
Naïve } simple, artless.
Net, neatly, clearly, plainly.
Noblement, impressively.

Noire, black note, crotchet.
Note sensible, the leading-note.
Nuances, lights and shades of expression.
Œuvre, work, composition.
Partition, a full score.
Pas, a dance; not.
Pathétique, pathetic.
Pédale, pedal.
Perlé, pearly, brilliant.
Peu à peu, little by little.
Plaintif, plaintive, doleful.
Plein jeu, the full power of the Organ.
Plus, more.
Plus allant, more moving, quicker.
Posément, steadily, sedately.
Pour, for.
Premier
Première } first.
Pressant, hurrying on.
Quatre, four.
Réduction, arrangement.
Refrain, the chorus or burden of a song.
Repos, a pause.
Reprise, the return of a previous passage of music.
Réjouissance, rejoicing.
Restez, remain.
Retenu, held back.
Réveillé, awakening, a military morning signal.
Romantique, romantic, imaginative.
Rythme ternaire, three-bar rhythm.
Sans, without.
Sec, dry, unornamented, staccato.
Serrez, press on.
Sonore, sonorous.
Soupir, a crotchet rest.
Sourdine, mute.
Soutenu, sustained.
Suite, a series of pieces connected in style.

Suivez, follow, attend, = *colla parte*.
Sur, on, upon, over.
Taille, the tenor part, the viola.
Temps, a beat.
Tendrement, tenderly, delicately.
Timbre, quality of tone or sound.
Ton, tone, tune, sound.
Touche, finger-board.
Très, very, most.

Triple croche, demisemiquaver.
Triste, sad.
Trois, three.
Un } one.
Une }
Un peu, a little.
Vif } lively, brisk.
Vive }
Vite } quickly, swiftly.
Vitement }
Voix, the voice.

161   GENERAL TERMS

Absolute Pitch. Definite pitch, the exact height or depth of a sound. The faculty of being able to sound or recognize the pitch of any sound without reference to a given note.

Accompaniment. That part of a composition which is subsidiary to a particular theme.

Acoustics. The science of sound.

Ad libitum (*Ad lib.*) (Lat.). At pleasure.

Air. Tune, song, melody.

Allemande. Often the first movement in a suite. It is in moderate $\frac{4}{4}$ time and generally begins with an unaccented note or a group of notes before the first strong beat, e.g. see Bach's 3rd English Suite.

Alto. The highest male voice. French name for viola.

Alto clef. See p. 4.

Anacrusis. One or more weak notes preceding the first accent of a phrase.

Anglaise. English Country Dance. A lively dance in $\frac{2}{4}$ or $\frac{3}{4}$ time, e.g. see Bach's 3rd French Suite.

Anticipation. The sounding of a note or chord before its natural and expected time.

Antiphon, Antiphony. Alternate singing, as between two portions of a choir.

Aria. A vocal or instrumental solo with accompaniment.

Arietta. A short Aria.

Arpa (see *Harp*).

Atonality. Absence of definite key.

Attendant keys (see *Relative keys*, p. 87).

Augmentation. Doubling the value of the notes in a melody, also the lengthening of a phrase by various rhythmic devices.

Authentic cadence. Perfect cadence (see p. 65).

Auxiliary note. An unessential note moving from a harmony note to the next above or below, and returning to the same harmony note.

Bagatelle. A trifle, a short piece of music.

Ballad. A popular song in which the chief feature is the singing of each verse to the same tune.

Baritone. The male voice whose range lies between that of the bass and tenor, approximately

Baritone clef. See p. 5.

Bass. The lowest male voice, with approximate compass

Bass Drum (see *Drum*).

Bass of chord. See par. 136, p. 61.

Bass Staff. See p. 3.

Basso continuo. A bass part with figures to indicate the harmony.

Basso ostinato (see *Ground-bass*, p. 82).

Bassoon (It. *Fagotto*). A double-reed instrument, the bass of the wood-wind family.

Bolero. A Spanish dance in ¾ time, founded on the rhythm

or e.g. Chopin, Op. 19.

Bourrée. A dance similar to the Gavotte, but beginning on the fourth crotchet of the bar, e.g. see Bach's 6th French Suite.

Brace. A sign } which joins two or more staves.

Bratsche (from Ital. *Viola da braccia*). The German name for the viola.

Burden. A refrain.

Cachuca (see *Bolero*).

Cacophony. Harsh or discordant harmony, bad or false intonation.

Cadence. See p. 65.

Cadenza. A florid part for solo instrument or voice, occurring generally towards the close of a composition, and often intended to exhibit the skill of the performer.

Canon. The strict imitation of a melody in another part at a certain interval of pitch and time.

Cantata. Originally a composition consisting of Recitatives and Arias to be sung by one voice, but now applied to short Oratorios or Operettas in which there is no action.

Canto fermo. Plain Chant. The given melody or fixed part in Counterpoint.

Cantus mensurabilis. Regular or measured melody.

Canzone. A song or ballad. Also applied to airs in two or three parts, containing passages of fugal imitation.

Catch. A species of round in humorous vein, so contrived that a different meaning is given by the singers 'catching' at each other's words.

Cavatina. A dramatic air, consisting of one section only.

Celesta. A small keyboard instrument in which the hammers strike small steel plates.

Chaconne. A set of variations on a ground-bass, generally in $\frac{3}{4}$ time, e.g. see Bach's 4th Sonata for Violin solo.

Chamber music. Originally applied to music performed in the salon or drawing-room, but now denoting ensemble instrumental music for two or more instruments in which each is of equal importance.

Choral. A service with music. A psalm or hymn tune.

Chorus. A composition to be sung by a body of singers. Also sometimes applied to a refrain.

Chromatic. Notes foreign to the key.

Chromatic Scale (see p. 34). Progresses by semitones only, so that five of the notes do not belong to the key.

Chromatic Semitone. One in which the two notes have the same letter-name, as F–F♯, so that both cannot belong to the same key.

Clarinet. A single-reed instrument of the wood-wind family.

Clavichord. A stringed instrument with a keyboard. The strings are struck by metal tangents.

Close harmony. Harmony in which the parts are kept as close together as possible.

Concert Overture. A single movement in classical form, not connected with any particular work, but written for concert performance.

Concerted music. Ensemble music, either vocal or instrumental, as distinct from solo.

Concerto (It.). (1) A concert; (2) a composition for one or more solo instruments with orchestra, modelled somewhat on the design of a Sonata.

Concertstück. A concert piece. A concerto on a smaller scale.

Contralto (counter alto). The lowest female voice. Approximate

compass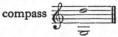

Contrary motion. The movement in opposite directions of two parts, i.e. one rising while the other falls.

Cor anglais (Fr.). The English horn, a double-reed instrument, the alto of the Oboe and Bassoon family.

Cornet (*Cornet-a-pistons*). A metal wind instrument of high pitch. It is often used in place of the Trumpet, as it is easier to play.

Counterpoint. The art of combining melodies.

Couplet. A figure of two notes slurred together. A duplet. Also a stanza or verse.

Courante. In a suite, the dance following the *Allemande*. There are two forms, French and Italian. The French courante is in $\frac{3}{2}$ time and slow tempo, the Italian courante in $\frac{3}{4}$ or $\frac{3}{8}$, with quick tempo and containing 'running' passages, e.g. see (1) Bach's 4th English Suite, (2) Bach's French Suites, nos. 5 and 6.

Cross-rhythm. Two or more parts moving together, each part in a different time.

Cue. See p. 58.

Cymbals (Ital. *Piatti*). Instruments of percussion consisting of two brass plates which are struck together.

Dampers. The mechanism of the pianoforte which checks the vibrations of the strings.

Deceptive cadence. Interrupted cadence (see p. 66).

Declamation. Dramatic singing as in recitatives, where the enunciation of the words is of greater importance than the melodic outline.

Diapason. (1) An octave; (2) the most important foundation stop of an organ.

Diatonic. Notes belonging to the key.

Diatonic scale (see p. 26). Progresses by tones and semitones, all the notes belonging to the key.

Diatonic semitone. One in which the two notes have different letter-names, as C-D♭, so that both can belong to the same key.

Diminution. Halving the value of the notes of a melody, also the shortening of a phrase by various rhythmic devices.

Dirge. A funeral song or march.

Dithyramb. A song in honour of Bacchus, hence a composition of a wild, impetuous character.

Divertimento. Composition in a pleasing style.

Division. Formerly a variation. A series of notes sung to one syllable.

Double. (1) Variation; (2) Chords (see p. 62).

Double-Bass. (Ital. *Contrabasso*). The lowest stringed instrument played with a bow. There are two kinds. (1) with three strings,

generally tuned to the notes (2) with four strings,

generally tuned thus The pitch is an octave lower than the written note.

Drum. An instrument of percussion. Drums are of different kinds. Those generally found in orchestras are : (1) Kettle-drums (Ital. *Timpani*). These are made of a shell of metal, across the mouth of which a membrane of parchment is stretched. By means of screws the membrane can be made tighter or slacker, so that sounds of definite pitch can be produced. (2) Big or Bass-drum (Ital. *Gran cassa*). This consists of a hollow cylinder, with a stretched membrane at each end. The pitch of the sounds cannot be changed in performance, and its use is principally to mark the rhythm. (3) Side or Snare drum (Ital. *Tamburo*). A small drum with two parchment heads, across one of which catgut strings are stretched to produce a rattling sound.

Elegy. A funeral or mournful song.

Enharmonic. See p. 8.

Enharmonic interval. The change in quality of an interval by an enharmonic change of notation, e.g. C-D♯, C-E♭.

Enharmonic key. Two scales having the same sounds with different notation, e.g. C♯ and D♭.

Enharmonic modulation. Change of key by enharmonically altering one or more notes of a chord.

Entr'acte. Music played by the orchestra between the acts of a play.

Episode. A theme or portion of a composition occurring but once, really a digression.

Equal temperament. The division of the octave into twelve equal parts or semitones.

Essential notes. The notes belonging to the harmony.

False cadence (see *Interrupted cadence*, p. 66). A cadence in which the dominant chord is followed by some other chord than the tonic.

False intonation. The production of notes not in correct pitch.

False relation. When a note occurring in a certain part of the harmony is found chromatically altered in a different part of the succeeding chord.

Fandango. A Spanish dance in ¾ time, e.g. see Gluck's Ballet *Don Juan*.

Figured bass. A bass part having figures added to indicate the harmony.

Flute (*Flauto traverso*). A wood-wind instrument in which the sound is produced by blowing across a hole near one end of the tube.

Fugato. In the style of a fugue.

Fughetta. A short fugue.

Fugue. A composition in contrapuntal style in which a certain subject is imitated in various parts according to certain rules.

Full score. A score containing all the parts of a vocal or instrumental work, each being written on a separate stave.

Fundamental tones. The tonic, dominant, and subdominant of the key.

Galliard. An old French dance in ¾ time and moderately quick tempo, used in conjunction with Pavan, e.g. see Byrd's ' Sir John Graye's Galliard '.

Gamut (Gamma). The scale.

Gavotte. An old French dance in 2/2 time which begins on the second beat of the bar (see *Musette*), e.g. see Bach's French Suite, No. 5.

Gigue. Generally the last movement in a suite. A lively dance, usually in 6/8 or 12/8 time, e.g. see Bach's French Suite, No. 6.

Glee. A vocal composition for three or more solo voices without accompaniment, generally of a cheerful nature, in which the several melodies run together without imitation.

Glockenspiel. An instrument made of bells or metal tubes, struck with hammers or by levers operated by a keyboard mechanism.

Ground-bass. A bass consisting of a few notes or bars, unceasingly repeated, and each time accompanied by a varied melody or harmony.

Half-cadence. An imperfect cadence (see p. 66), i.e. a close on the dominant.

Harmonics, or upper partials. Overtones accompanying a fundamental tone, produced by the dividing up of the vibrating string or column of air into its aliquot parts.

Harmony (see p. 59). The combination of musical sounds.

Harp (Ital. *Arpa*). An instrument consisting of a triangular frame, with gut or wire strings which are plucked by the fingers.

Harpsichord. A stringed instrument generally with two keyboards. The strings are plucked by quills attached to the ends of slips of wood called jacks.

Heptachord. A scale of seven sounds.

Hexachord. A scale of six sounds.

Homophony. Unison. Several voices or instruments in unison.

Horn (Ital. *Corno*). A brass wind instrument made of a long tube curved to form a circle, bell-shaped at one end, and with a cupped mouth at the other.

Hornpipe. An old English dance in $\frac{4}{4}$ time (formerly in triple time), e.g. see Arne's *King Arthur*.

Imitation. The repetition of a theme or figure announced in one part by another part, not necessarily according to strict laws, as in a Canon or Fugue.

Imperfect cadence (see p. 66). A cadence ending on the dominant preceded by some other chord.

Imperfect consonances. The major and minor thirds and sixths (see p. 40).

Impromptu. A piece in the style of an improvisation.

Infinite canon. An endless canon in which the end joins on to the beginning without stopping.

Inganno. A deception. Interrupted cadence.

Interlude. A tune or movement played or sung between the acts or scenes of a drama, or a passage occurring between two sections of a melody.

Intermezzo. An interlude played between the acts of an opera, or a light piece introduced between two of a more serious nature.

Interrupted cadence. A cadence in which the dominant chord is followed by some other chord than the tonic, such as the submediant (see *False cadence*).

Intonation. The production of musical sounds by voice or instrument.

Invention. A suite; a composition of a fanciful character.

Inversion. Of melody. Changing the direction of the progression of the notes, ascending intervals becoming descending, and vice versa, e.g.

Of chords (see p. 61). Of intervals (see p. 41).

Just intonation. The production of musical sounds in perfect tune.

Key. The relationship of all the notes of a scale to the tonic or key-note.

Lay. A short light air.

Leitmotive. A leading motive; a short musical theme intended to represent some idea or character.

Libretto. The book of words set to music as an opera or extended vocal composition.

Loure. An old French dance, generally in $\frac{6}{4}$ time, e.g. see Bach's French Suite, No. 5.

Madrigal. An unaccompanied secular composition for three or more voices, with free imitation in the parts.

Mastersinger. } A title given to the most noted musician of a district
Meistersinger. } in Germany during the Middle Ages. The meistersingers formed themselves into musical guilds about the beginning of the fourteenth century. Candidates for membership were admitted only after a severe test of their knowledge of the rules of composition established by the guilds.

Mazurka. A Polish dance in fairly quick $\frac{3}{4}$ time, generally having an accent on the second beat of the bar, e.g. Chopin's *Mazurkas.*

Melody. A progression of single sounds of different pitch.

Metronome. A machine, or pendulum, with a graded scale for measuring the tempo, e.g. M.M. (Maelzel's metronome) 60 = 60 beats per minute.

Minuet. A stately dance in $\frac{3}{4}$ (or sometimes $\frac{3}{8}$) time. Often a second minuet in a different key was played alternately with the first. This second minuet was called the Trio, e.g. see Bach's *Partita*, No. 1.

Mixed cadence. Dominant chord preceded by subdominant chord.

Mixture, or Compound stop. An organ stop having two or more ranks of pipes.

Mode. A scale consisting of an alphabetical progression of tones and semitones (see chap. 5).

Modulation. Change of key.

Morris dance. An old English dance in $\frac{4}{4}$ time.

Motet. An unaccompanied vocal composition in contrapuntal style.

Musette. A dance in $\frac{4}{4}$ time on a drone bass, generally used alternately with the Gavotte, e.g. see Bach's English Suite, No. 3.

Muta. Change. In music for brass instruments, change of crook. Different tuning of the drum.

Mute. A device for softening the tone of an instrument.

Natural keys. Those requiring no signature, as C major and A minor. The white keys of a pianoforte or organ.

Natural Modulation. Change to a nearly related key (see *RelativeKeys*).

Nocturne (Fr.). } 'A night piece', a piece of quiet character.
Notturno (It.). }

Nonetto (It.). A composition for nine voices or instruments.

Notation. The art of writing music by signs—notes, rests, &c.

Oboe. A double-reed wood-wind instrument.

Octet. } A composition for eight voices or instruments.
Octuor (Fr.). }

Open harmony. Where the parts or voices are more or less equidistant from each other.

Open note. A note on an unstopped string of a violin or other stringed instrument; on the horn and trumpet, one produced without the use of valves.

Open Score. See p. 5.

Opera. A term generally used for a secular drama set to music for voices and instruments, with scenery, action, &c.

Opera-Buffa (It.). A comic opera.

Opus. Work, composition.

Oratorio. A sacred drama set to music for voices and instruments, performed without scenery or action.

Organ point. A long sustained note, which may or may not be an essential note of the accompanying harmony. If it occurs in an upper part it is said to be inverted.

Overture. An orchestral introduction to an opera or oratorio (see *Concert Overture*).

Paean. A hymn of triumph.

Part. The music for each separate voice or instrument.

Part-writing. Harmony in which the melodic nature of each part is considered.

Partita. An old term for variation, also a suite.

Partition (Fr.).
Partitur (Ger.). } A full score for voices or instruments, or
Partitura (It.). } a combination of both.

Passacaglia (It.). ⎰ Originally a dance in triple time constructed on
Passacaille (Fr.). ⎱ a Ground-bass. Bach used the form in his Passacaglia and Fugue in C minor for organ.

Passepied. An old French dance in quick $\frac{3}{4}$ or $\frac{3}{8}$ time, e.g. see Bach's *Partita in B minor*.

Passing notes. Notes which do not belong to the harmony, but pass by step from one harmony note to another.

Pastel. A term borrowed from painting, to describe a short piece of music of an atmospheric nature.

Pastorale. A short movement in a pastoral or rural style.

Pavan (Eng.).
Pavana (It.). } A slow dance in simple duple or quadruple time, e.g.
Pavane (Fr.). } see Bull's 'Lord Lumley's Pavan'.

Pedal. A piece of wood or metal to be pressed down by the foot. (1) On the pianoforte there are usually two pedals, one which is used to soften the tone, and the other to remove the dampers and sustain the tone. (2) On the harp the pedals are used to sharpen or make natural one note of the scale throughout the compass of the instrument. (3) On the organ there are two kinds of pedal, one for altering the combination of stops, and the other forming a keyboard for the feet.

Pedale (It.). }
Pedal point. } See *Organ point*.

Pentatonic scale. See p. 36.

Percussion. Striking. Instruments of percussion are of two kinds. (1) Those which produce a note of definite pitch, e.g. Kettle-drum, Glockenspiel. (2) Those which merely produce a noise, e.g. Bass-drum, Cymbals. The term is also applied to the 'Action' of the pianoforte.

Perfect cadence. See p. 65.

Period. A musical sentence. The shortest statement which is complete in itself.

Per recte et retro. Forward, then backward. The notes of a melody reversed, e.g.

Phrase. A division of a musical sentence, generally ending with some form of cadence.

Phrasing. Musical punctuation. The rhythmical grouping of the notes of a melody.

Phrygian cadence. One ending with a major chord on the mediant in a major key, the bass note generally approached by step from the note above or below (see end of third line of hymn-tune 'St. Anne').

Pianoforte score. One with each voice part on a separate stave with its proper clef, and the accompaniment arranged for the pianoforte.

Piatti. See *Cymbals.*

Piccolo. A small flute sounding an octave higher than the ordinary flute.

Plagal cadence. See p. 66.

Plain chant. See *Canto Fermo.*

Plectrum. A quill or piece of wood used to pluck the strings of the Mandoline, &c.

Polacca. See *Polonaise.*

Polka. A Bohemian dance in quick $\frac{2}{4}$ time, with the third quaver accented.

Polonaise or *Polacca.* A Polish dance in $\frac{3}{4}$ time and moderate tempo, the cadences occurring on the second and third beats of the bar, e.g. Chopin's *Polonaises.*

Polyphony. Music written for many parts.

Polytonality. The simultaneous use of two or more keys.

Ponticello (It.). The bridge of a stringed instrument such as the violin, violoncello, &c.

Portamento (It. = carrying). The term now generally applied to gliding from one note to another in singing, violin playing, &c. Also a term for mezzo-staccato.

Pot-pourri (Fr.). A connected medley of tunes or fragments of tunes.

Preparation. The appearance of a dissonant note of a chord in the same part in the previous chord.

Progression. The movement from note to note or from chord to chord.

Provençales. Poets or troubadours of Provence in the eleventh century.

Punctum contra punctum (Lat.). Point against point. Counterpoint.

Quartet. A composition for four voices or instruments.

Quintet. A composition for five voices or instruments.

Quintuple time. Five beats in a bar, e.g. $\frac{5}{4}$, $\frac{15}{8}$.

Recitativo parlante. } Unaccompanied recit., or accompanied by simple
Recitativo secco. } chords.

Recitativo accompagnato. } Accompanied recit.
Recitativo stromentato. }

Register. The compass of a voice or instrument. The divisions of the vocal compass—head, middle, chest.

Relative keys. Those keys having most notes in common. The relative keys to a major are the Dominant and Subdominant major, and the three relative minors, i.e. Submediant, Mediant, and Supertonic minor. The relative keys to a minor are the Dominant and Subdominant minors and the three relative majors, i.e. the Mediant, flattened Leading-note, and the Submediant majors, e.g.:

Keys related to C major		*Keys related to C minor*	
Tonic C major . .	A minor.	Tonic C minor .	E♭ major.
Dom. G major . .	E minor.	Dom. G minor .	B♭ major.
Subdom. F major	D minor.	Subdom. F minor	A♭ major.

Resolution. The progression of a dissonant note or chord to another which may be consonant or dissonant.

Resonance. Sound, reverberation.

Retardation. A suspension which resolves upwards.

Retrograde imitation. Where the imitative part reverses the order of the notes in the part imitated.

Rhapsody. A composition in the style of a fantasia, often with no definite form.

Rhythm. See p. 65.

Ricercare (It.=sought after). A composition exhibiting technical skill.

Rigaudon. An old French dance of a lively nature in quick $\frac{4}{4}$ time, e.g. see Rameau's *Dardanus.*

Ripieno. The tutti, as distinguished from the solo groups.

Ritmo di tre battute. Three-bar rhythm.

Ritornello. Symphony or interlude in a song.

Rondeau (Fr.). } A composition in which the theme appears at least
Rondo (It.). } three times, interspersed by material of a contrasting nature.

Roulade. A vocal cadenza.

Round. A vocal composition in three or more parts, in the form of an infinite canon at the unison.

Salterello. A lively dance in $\frac{6}{8}$ time, with the first and fourth quavers dotted.

Sarabande. A slow stately dance in $\frac{3}{4}$ or $\frac{3}{8}$ time, generally following the courante in the suite. It has a strong accent on the second beat of the bar, e.g. Handel's *Lascia ch'io pianga*.

Scena (It.).
Scene (Fr.). } A scene, or portion of an operatic act. An operatic vocal solo of a dramatic nature, generally consisting of a recitative and aria.

Scherzo. A development of the minuet, the form being much extended and the tempo quickened; see examples by Chopin, Mendelssohn, &c. Beethoven used it in many of his Sonatas and Symphonies in place of the Minuet.

Score. The whole vocal and instrumental parts of a composition, written on separate staves.

Septet. A composition for seven voices or instruments.

Septuple time. Seven beats in a bar, e.g. $\frac{7}{4}$, $\frac{21}{8}$.

Sequence. The repetition of a figure of melody or harmony at a different pitch.

Serenade. 'Evening music'.

Siciliano. A graceful dance in $\frac{6}{8}$ or $\frac{12}{8}$ time, e.g. see Bach's 5th Violin Sonata in G minor.

Similar motion. The parts rising or falling together, i.e. moving in the same direction.

Solo. Alone. Music to be played or sung by one performer only, with or without accompaniment.

Sonata. A term formerly applied to an instrumental piece as opposed to a vocal one. It is now a composition consisting of several movements constructed according to certain rules of design. The same plan of construction is common to symphonies, instrumental trios, quartets, &c.

Sonata da camera. A chamber sonata.

Sonata da chiesa. A church (organ) sonata.

Sonatina. Originally a short easy sonata, but the term is applied to short sonatas quite independent of their difficulty.

Soprano. Highest female voice, compass approximately

Soprano clef. See p. 4.

Spinet, see *Virginal*.

Stanza. A verse of a song.

Stop. (1) A register or row of pipes in an organ, and the knob or tablet which controls the admission of wind to the pipes. (2) In stringed instruments, the pressure of the finger on the string.

Stretto. In fugue, a part where subject and answer overlap. (Also see p. 72.)

Subject. A leading or principal theme.

Super. Above, over.

Suspension. The retention of one or more notes of a chord into the succeeding one.

Symphony. A composition of several movements scored for full orchestra, constructed on the same plan as a sonata.

Syncopation. See p. 21.

Tambourin. A French dance in quick $\frac{2}{4}$ time, e.g. see Rameau's *Pièce de clavecin* in A.

Tarantella. An Italian dance in quick $\frac{6}{8}$ time, e.g. Chopin, Op. 43.

Temperament. The method of tuning the sounds of a scale. See *Equal* and *Unequal temperament.*

Tenor (Lat. *Tenere,* to hold). High male voice with compass approximately the lowest note of which is called Tenor C. Originally the chief melody or 'holding' part was given to the Tenor. The name is also given to the Viola and many other instruments having about the same compass.

Tenor clef. See p. 4.

Tessitura. Web, texture.

Thorough bass. Figured bass. The art of denoting harmonies by placing figures over or under a bass part.

Tierce de Picardie. A major chord ending a piece in a minor key (see p. 67).

Toccata (It. = touched). A brilliant piece in the form of an improvisation.

Tonality. The relationship of all the sounds of a scale to the tonic or key-note, and the relationship of key to key where changed by modulation.

Transient modulation. A temporary or passing modulation.

Transitional dominant. The dominant chord used in a transient or passing modulation.

Transposition. Changing the pitch, key, or mode of a piece.

Treble. (1) The highest vocal or instrumental part, which generally contains the melody. (2) Treble or Soprano, the highest voice of women or boys. (3) Staff (see p. 3).

Trepak. A Russian dance, e.g. see Tschaikowski's *Casse-Noisette.*

Triangle. A steel rod bent into the shape of a triangle. It is held by a string and struck by a ' beater ', generally made of metal.

Trio. A composition for three performers.

Tritone. An interval of three tones, an augmented 4th.

Trombone. A brass wind instrument, made in different sizes, called Alto, Tenor, and Bass, the alto one being nearly obsolete. It consists of two tubes, one of which slides in and out of the other, so that a single tube is formed which can be lengthened or shortened at will, thus producing notes of varying pitch.

Trumpet (Ital. *Tromba*). A brass wind instrument of high pitch, with a virile and penetrating tone.

Tuba. A brass wind instrument of wide bore, the lowest of the brass family.

Tune. Air, or melody.

Tutti (It.). All. A passage for all the performers.

Unequal temperament. The method of tuning the twelve sounds included in the octave, by which the scales having few sharps or flats are more in tune than the others.

Unessential notes. Notes which do not belong to the chord.

Unison. Two or more parts sounding the same pitch. (See p. 37.)

Upper Partials. See *Harmonics*.

Valse, Waltz. A graceful dance in moderate ¾ time.

Variation. A modification or elaboration of a theme by various devices.

Violin (Ital. *Violino*). An instrument of four strings tuned to the notes and played with a bow.

Viola (Ital. *Viola da braccia*, Fr. *Alto*). A larger size of violin tuned to the notes . The tenor of the ordinary String Quartet.

Violoncello (Ital.). Generally abbreviated to 'Cello. An instrument of four strings tuned and played with a bow. It is the bass of the ordinary String Quartet.

Virginal (or *Pair of Virginals*). A keyed instrument similar to the Spinet, differing only in shape and the arrangement of the strings. It is oblong, with the keys placed at the side, the Spinet being wing-shaped like the modern grand piano. In both instruments the strings are sounded by means of a plectrum of leather or quill.

Vocal score. See *Pianoforte score*.

Vox. The voice.

Waltz. See *Valse*.

CHAPTER 10

HINTS ON VARIOUS SUBJECTS

Changing a passage from Simple to Compound Time (or vice versa)

162. Bear in mind the following:

(1) That all regular divisions of the beat in simple time become irregular in compound time, e.g.

(2) That irregular groups in simple time such as triplets and sextolets (which are really groupings borrowed from compound time) become regular when written in compound time, e.g.

Therefore in re-writing in compound time a passage such as the following—

Ex. 121.   (a)   (b)   (c)

the point to observe is that whereas here there are three crotchet beats in the bar, the corresponding compound time will be three dotted crotchet beats, having a time-signature of $\frac{9}{8}$, so that each beat shown above as a crotchet now becomes a dotted crotchet:

Ex. 122.   (a)   (b)   (c)

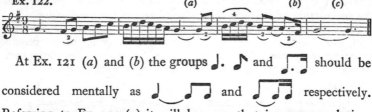

At Ex. 121 (a) and (b) the groups   and   should be considered mentally as   and   respectively.

Referring to Ex. 122 (a) it will be seen that in compound time the ♩ has become a dotted crotchet, and the group of two quavers a duplet (see rule 1 of above), whereas at (b) the dotted quaver and semiquaver group has become a duplet, being together equal to a group of two quavers.

At (c) as there is no note which can represent a whole bar in compound triple time (see p. 20) the ♩. must be taken as

This in $\frac{9}{8}$ time becomes ♩. ♩.

A similar method is adopted in changing from compound to simple time, e.g. $\frac{12}{16}$ would become $\frac{4}{8}$.

Finding the Time of a given Passage

163. (1) Generally the manner in which the notes and rests are grouped will be a sufficient guide, e.g.

Ex. 123.

In bar 1 each group of notes is equal in value to one crotchet, therefore the crotchet is the beat. It will be seen that there is the equivalent of four crotchets in each bar, so that the time-signature is $\frac{4}{4}$.

(2) Be careful to note whether a rest forms the commencement or completion of a beat, e.g.

Ex. 124.   (a)   (b)

At (a) the ♪· should be noted and the group of three semiquavers (= ♪·) Thus the beat is a ♪· and the semiquaver rest is the beginning of the second beat, therefore the time-signature is $\frac{9}{16}$.

At (b) the crotchet should be noted and the group of two quavers (= ♪) Thus the beat is a ♪ and the semiquaver rest is the completion of the first beat, therefore the time-signature is $\frac{3}{4}$.

(3) Generally speaking, the presence of a triplet or sextolet indicates simple time (for such divisions are regular in compound time) and the presence of a duplet or quadruplet indicates compound time (for such divisions are regular in simple time), e.g.

Ex. 125.   (a)   (b)

At (a) the triplet and the sextolet each equal a ♪ and there is the equivalent of four crotchets in the bar, so that the time-signature is $\frac{4}{4}$.

At (*b*) the duplet and quadruplet each equal a ♩. and there is the equivalent of four dotted crotchets in the bar, so that the time-signature is $\frac{12}{8}$.

Finding the Key of a Diatonic Passage

164. (1) (*a*) If the passage contains sharp accidentals only (i.e. no flats are present) find which sharp is last in order (see p. 28). This is generally the seventh degree of the scale (see p. 27) and therefore the key-note will be a semitone above. Then, according as the third degree of the scale, occurring in the passage, is a major or minor 3rd from the key-note, so is the passage major or minor (the reason being that the 3rd degree of a minor scale is one semitone lower than the 3rd degree of its tonic major), e.g.

Ex. 126.

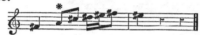

Here the last sharp in the order of sharps is E♯, therefore the key-note is F♯. The 3rd degree from F♯ occurring in the passage at * is A, and that is a minor 3rd above F♯, so that the key is F♯ minor.

(*b*) If a double sharp is present, it may generally be accepted as the 7th note of a minor scale, for the presence of such a note implies that an already sharpened note has been raised, and it is only in a minor scale that this occurs, e.g.

Ex. 127.

F× is the 7th note of the scale, therefore the key is G♯ minor.

(2) If in a passage containing flats, a sharp occurs, it may be accepted as the 7th degree of a minor, for only in a minor scale do sharps and flats occur together (indeed this can apply to only two minor scales, G and D), e.g.

Ex. 128.

F♯ is the 7th note of the scale, therefore the key is G minor.

(3) (*a*) If the passage contains flat accidentals only (i.e. no sharps

are present) find which flat is last in order (see p. 28). Now see if all the flats up to that one (in order) are present, and if so, the passage will be in the major key of which the last flat is the 4th degree (see p. 28), e.g.

Ex. 129.

The last flat (in order) is D♭ and all the other flats B♭, E♭, A♭ are present, there-fore the key is A♭ major.

(*b*) Frequently, however, it will be found that one flat is missing, and if so, it is generally the 7th degree of a minor scale, for this implies that a flat note has been raised, and only in a minor scale does this occur (see p. 32), e.g.

Ex. 130.

The last flat in order is G♭, but all the flats up to that one are not present, only B♭ E♭ — D♭ G♭ being found. That is, A♭ has been raised and A is therefore the 7th note of the minor scale of B♭.

NOTE.—In the following passage it would appear that more than one flat is missing:

Ex. 131.

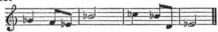

The last flat is C♭, but it will be seen that A♭ is missing, and D♭ is raised (B♭ E♭ — — G♭ C♭). However, the note A♭ should be disregarded entirely, for, not being present at all in the passage, it is not essential to the establishment of the key, and if it did occur in the passage, would be flattened. Thus the raised flat is D, so that the key is E♭ minor.

Finding the key of a passage containing Chromatic notes

165. Generally speaking, in melodic writing chromatic notes are used as lower (and occasionally upper) auxiliary notes (see p. 78) to the diatonic notes. They can usually be recognized by the fact that, though they are often approached by leap from the previous note, they almost invariably rise or fall a semitone to a note of the scale.

In the following passages, consisting of the scales of C major and A minor with an auxiliary note below each degree, all the sharpened notes are chromatic with the exception of the G♯ (se) and F♯ (ba) of the minor scale:

Ex. 132. (a)

d t, d r de r m re m f m f s fe s l se l t le t d'

(b)

l se l t le t d' t d' r' de' r' m' re' m' f' m' f' se' ba' se' l'

The two passages should be repeatedly played over with and without the accidentals (retaining of course the G♯ and F♯ of the minor scale), until the mental effect of the chromatic notes has been fully realized.

Ex. 133. (a)

m re m d s, s f m de r t,

(b)

t, d se, t, l, t, m re m f m de r

At (a) D♭ is the last in the order of flats, and is therefore the fourth degree of the scale. As the third degree C is major the passage is in the key of A♭ major; and B♮ is a chromatic auxiliary to C, and A♮ a chromatic auxiliary to B♭.

At (b) the last sharp in order is B♯, but this is contradicted later by B♮, which will be felt to be a more important note. Taking E♯, the next sharp in order, as the 7th degree, and A♮ and D♮ as the 3rd and 6th degrees of the scale, we find the passage to be in the key of F♯ minor, with B♯ as chromatic auxiliary to C♯, and A♯ as chromatic auxiliary to B.

Transposition

166. Proceed as follows:

(1) Find the key of the passage, noting whether major or minor.

(2) Note the interval above or below to which it is to be transposed, and then find the new key by calculating the required interval (here remember to retain the mode, whether major or minor).

(3) Note on which degree of the scale it commences, and begin on the same degree of the new key.

(4) Remember that all accidentals do not necessarily retain the same form in the new key. Thus a ♯ means that a note has been raised and may become a ♮ or x, a ♭ means that a note has been lowered and may become a ♮ or ♭♭, a ♮ means that a note has been raised or lowered and may become a ♯ or ♭.

e.g. Transpose this passage up a diminished 5th, using Treble staff:

Ex. 134.

(1) The key is B minor. (2) A diminished 5th above is F minor. (3) It commences on the tonic B, therefore the transposed version will begin on the new tonic F. (4) All the accidental ♯'s become ♮'s, thus:

Ex. 135.

Sometimes no key-signature is given. The procedure, however, is the same, but it must be borne in mind which notes belong to the key-signature and which are shown by accidentals.

e.g. Transpose the following passage down a minor 6th, prefixing the proper key-signature and using the Alto staff:

Ex. 136.

The passage is in the key of A♭ minor. As it is written without key-signature the F and G (6th and 7th degrees) in bar 2 do not require accidentals. In the transposed version with key-signature the corresponding notes require accidentals, thus:

Ex. 137.

167. Sometimes, in addition to change of key, a change of *mode* is required. Again the method is the same as before, but it must be remembered that if the given passage is major it will become minor, and vice versa. Suppose we are asked to transpose the following passage into the minor key a perfect 4th higher, using the treble staff and prefixing the proper key-signature:

Ex. 138.

Adopting the method already given, it will be seen that the given passage being in A major, the new key is D minor. It must be remembered, however, that the melodic minor should be used (i.e. in descending by step from tonic to dominant the minor 7th and 6th are required, and in ascending by step from dominant to tonic, the major 6th and 7th are required).

Thus in the solution below (bar 1) C♮ and B♭ are actually only a diminished 4th above G♯ and F♯ (bar 1 above), but this is of no significance, for the notes characteristic of the minor mode must be used. In bar 2 below, the major 6th and 7th are used:

Ex. 139.

A similar method is adopted in changing from minor to major, i.e. notes characteristic of the minor key must be altered to those characteristic of the major key.

Transference from Close or Short Score to Open Score

168. In transferring a passage from close to open score (see p. 5) care must be taken with regard to the insertion of accidentals. In open score each line must be treated independently. In the second bar of the following extract there is an E♯ in the Alto part which occurs later in the Treble, and a G♯ in the Treble which occurs later in the Alto. In close score it is not necessary to repeat the accidentals, as both notes are of the same pitch and in the same bar, but in open score the sharps must be inserted in both parts.

Care must also be taken in regard to the direction of the stems (see p. 10) and to the proper spacing of the notes, so that those played together are placed directly under one another.

Ex. 140.

(a)   Piano or Close Score.   BACH.

(b)   Open Score with C clefs.

(c)   String Quartet.

Vln. 1.

Vln. 2.

Viola.

'Cello.

SET IN GREAT BRITAIN
AT THE
UNIVERSITY PRESS
OXFORD
REPRINTED FROM PLATES
BY NEILL AND CO. LTD.
EDINBURGH